FOOTBALL LEGENDS

Troy Aikman

Terry Bradshaw

Jim Brown

Dan Marino

Joe Montana

Joe Namath

Walter Payton

Jerry Rice

Barry Sanders

Deion Sanders

Emmitt Smith

Steve Young

CHELSEA HOUSE PUBLISHERS

TERRY BRADSHAW

Ron Frankl

Introduction by
Chuck Noll

CHELSEA HOUSE PUBLISHERS
New York · Philadelphia

Produced by Daniel Bial and Associates
New York, New York.

Picture research by Alan Gottlieb
Cover illustration by Jon Weiman

3 5 7 9 8 6 4

Frankl, Ron.
    Terry Bradshaw / Ron Frankl.
      p. cm. — (Football legends)
    Includes bibliographical references and index.
    ISBN 0-7910-2451-2 (hard)
    1. Bradshaw, Terry—Juvenile literature. 2. Football players-United
States—Biography—Juvenile literature. 3. National Football
League—Juvenile literature. [1. Bradshaw, Terry, 1954– .
    2. Football players. I. Title. II. Series.
GV939.B68F73 1994
796.332'092—dc20
    [B]   94-5780
                                                                  CIP
                                                                   AC

CONTENTS

A WINNING ATTITUDE

Chuck Noll

Don't ever fall into the trap of believing, "I could never do that. And I won't even try—I don't want to embarrass myself." After all, most top athletes had no idea what they could accomplish when they were young. A secret to the success of every star quarterback and sure-handed receiver is that they tried. If they had not tried, if they had not persevered, they would never have discovered how far they could go and how much they could achieve.

You can learn about trying hard and overcoming challenges by being a sports fan. Or you can take part in organized sports at any level, in any capacity. The student messenger at my high school is now president of a university. A reserve ballplayer who got very little playing time in high school now owns a very successful business. Both of them benefited by the lesson of perseverance that sports offers. The main point is that you don't have to be a Hall of Fame athlete to reap the benefits of participating in sports.

In math class, I learned that the whole is equal to the sum of its parts. But that is not always the case when you are dealing with people. Sports has taught me that the whole is either greater than or less than the sum of its parts, depending on how well the parts work together. And how the parts work together depends on how they really understand the concept of teamwork.

Most people believe that teamwork is a fifty-fifty proposition. But true teamwork is seldom, if ever, fifty-fifty. Teamwork is *whatever it takes to get the job done.* There is no time for the measurement of contributions, no time for anything but concentrating on your job.

One year, my Pittsburgh Steelers were playing the Houston Oilers in the Astrodome late in the season, with the division championship on the line. Our offensive line was hard hit by the flu, our starting quarterback was out with an injury, and we were having difficulty making a first down. There was tremendous pressure on our defense to perform well—and they rose to the occasion. If the players on the defensive unit had been measuring their contribution against the offense's contribution, they would have given up and gone home. Instead, with a "whatever it takes" attitude, they increased their level of concentration and performance, forced turnovers, and got the ball into field goal range for our offense. Thanks to our defense's winning attitude, we came away with a victory.

Believing in doing whatever it takes to get the job done is what separates a successful person from someone who is not as successful. Nobody can give you this winning outlook; you have to develop it. And I know from experience that it can be learned and developed on the playing field.

My favorite people on the football field have always been offensive linemen and defensive backs. I say this because it takes special people to perform well in jobs in which there is little public recognition when they are doing things right but are thrust into the spotlight as soon as they make a mistake. That is exactly what happens to a lineman whose man sacks the quarterback or a defensive back who lets his receiver catch a touchdown pass. They know the importance of being part of a group that believes in teamwork and does not point fingers at one another.

Sports can be a learning situation as much as it can be fun. And that's why I say, "Get involved. Participate."

CHUCK NOLL, the Pittsburgh Steelers head coach from 1969–1991, led his team to four Super Bowl victories—the most by any coach. Widely respected as an innovator on both offense and defense, Noll was inducted into the Pro Football Hall of Fame in 1993.

1

THE COMEBACK

For Terry Bradshaw, it was the lowest moment of his football career. While the 25-year-old quarterback of the Pittsburgh Steelers could take great satisfaction in having played a major role in leading the Steelers to the playoffs the previous two seasons, Bradshaw began the 1974 season on the sidelines. To his tremendous disappointment, the young quarterback had been relegated to second-string status by Coach Chuck Noll. The demotion had left Bradshaw hurt and confused, unsure of his future with the Steelers.

Bradshaw stood 6'3" and weighed 210 pounds, was a good runner, and was blessed with a powerful and accurate throwing arm. No one could question his physical abilities. But coaches, players, sportswriters, and fans wondered whether Terry Bradshaw had the intelli-

In 1974, Bradshaw was in his fourth pro season. Although the Steelers had become a much better team in that time, Bradshaw clearly was not a dominating quarterback—yet.

gence and personality to succeed in the NFL.

Despite flashes of brilliance, Bradshaw's performance on the field had been disappointing. He often seemed nervous during games, and his teammates said that he sometimes had difficulty selecting the best plays during team huddles. He was easily confused by opposing defenses and was often unable to make the quick and correct decision that was necessary to make the play successful.

While Bradshaw conquered his nervousness as his career progressed, he would still become flustered occasionally and make major mistakes at critical points in a game. When pressured by the other team's pass rushers, he appeared to panic and would either throw the ball too early or attempt to throw a pass to a receiver who was well covered by the defense. These poorly chosen passes were often intercepted.

Interceptions were a major problem for Bradshaw. During his five-year career he had thrown far more interceptions than touchdown passes, much to the frustration of his coaches and teammates.

Coach Noll and the Pittsburgh coaching staff grew unhappy with Bradshaw's inconsistency.

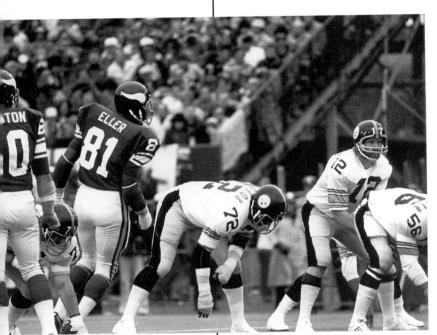

Minnesota Vikings defensive lineman Carl Eller was looking forward to crushing Bradshaw in the 1975 Super Bowl so much that he was offsides on this play.

They questioned his leadership capabilities, as well as his commitment to improving his skills. Noll decided that the Steelers' offense might be better off with another field leader. Before the beginning of the 1974 season, Noll named Joe Gilliam, a second-year player, as the team's starting quarterback.

Bradshaw was deeply disappointed to be on the sidelines. He requested a trade to another team where he would have the opportunity to play. The Steelers ignored his request. Bradshaw had no alternative except to wait and hope for another chance to prove himself on the field. "I thought my career may be at an end," Bradshaw recalled later. "Confidence-wise, you couldn't go any lower."

For Bradshaw, the benching was the low-point of his career, but he later recognized its value as a turning point in his development as a quarterback. "I hated that feeling I was going through. I didn't ever want to experience it again. It made me tougher. It made me appreciate the job. It made me appreciate my ability as a quarterback. It made me work harder."

The Steelers performed inconsistently with Gilliam as the starting quarterback. By the ninth game of the season, Bradshaw was given the chance to regain the starting job. He returned to the lineup a changed and improved player. He seemed determined to prove to everyone that he belonged as Pittsburgh's quarterback. For the first time in his Steeler career, Bradshaw displayed the self-confidence and dedication necessary to be a successful quarterback.

Bradshaw reduced the number of mistakes he made on the field and played with an intensity and consistency that he had not shown in the past. He was determined to make a major contribution to his team's success. With Bradshaw back in the starting lineup, the Steelers' offense revived. They won four of their last six games and captured the American Football Conference (AFC) Central Division title, qualifying for the playoffs for the third consecutive season.

The Steelers demolished the Buffalo Bills and the Oakland Raiders in the first two rounds of the playoffs, due largely to the inspired play of Pittsburgh's overpowering defense, which was nicknamed the "Steel Curtain" and was led by such standouts as defensive ends Mean Joe Greene and L. C. Greenwood and linebackers Jack Ham and Jack Lambert.

Bradshaw played well in both contests, throwing a touchdown pass in each game, but the offensive hero in each game was running back Franco Harris, the Steelers' powerful rusher. With these two victories, the Steelers captured their first AFC title and earned their first trip to the Super Bowl. After five often frustrating seasons, Bradshaw had finally earned the opportunity to lead his team to its first National Football League championship.

On the day of the Super Bowl, Bradshaw was more nervous than usual, but he had every reason to be anxious. The 25-year-old quarterback was about to take the field for his first appearance in the Super Bowl, football's biggest game. It was January 12, 1975, and a crowd of nearly 81,000 fans filled Tulane Stadium in New Orleans, Louisiana, for Super Bowl IX. Another 78 million viewers watched the game on television.

It was a chilly day in New Orleans as Super Bowl IX began. From the opening minutes, the game was a defensive struggle, with the Steel

The Steelers' 1975 Super Bowl victory was in good part due to the running of Franco Harris. Here he scores a touchdown as Jackie Wallace is too late for the tackle.

Curtain meeting its match in the Vikings' strong defense. The Vikings' defensive unit was almost as talented as Pittsburgh's, featuring such standouts as Jim Marshall, Carl Eller, and Alan Page, who had been the first defensive player ever voted the NFL's most valuable player.

The Viking offense, led by quarterback Fran Tarkenton and running back Chuck Foreman, had great difficulty moving the ball downfield, but so did the Steeler offense. Neither team scored in the first quarter of the game. The Steelers missed on one field goal attempt and mishandled a second try, and the Vikings missed a field goal as well.

In the first half, Bradshaw and the Steelers had only 15 passing yards and 64 rushing yards, while Minnesota was held to 20 yards on passes and a surprising total of 0 yards on the ground. The only score of the half occurred when Minnesota fumbled the ball in their own end zone on a running play. The Vikings fell on the fumble, and the result was a safety for the Steelers. The tally at half-time—Pittsburgh 2, Minnesota 0—seemed more like a baseball than a football score.

The second half was only a few seconds old when Minnesota's Bill Brown fumbled the kick-off and the Steelers recovered on the Vikings' 30 yardline. Bradshaw called four consecutive running plays and, on the last, Franco Harris burst into the end zone on a nine-yard sweep. Steeler kicker Roy Gerela was successful on the point-after attempt. The score was now 9-0.

The defensive struggle continued, and the Vikings' first score came early in the fourth quarter, when they blocked a Steeler punt near the Pittsburgh goal line and recovered the ball in the end zone for a touchdown. Minnesota missed the extra point, and the Steelers held a 9-6 lead.

There were more than 10 minutes left in the game as the Vikings kicked off—plenty of time for the Vikings to get the ball back and score if Pittsburgh's offense could be stopped. The Steelers took over on their own 34 yardline. Bradshaw engineered a brilliant drive, designed not only to score but also to use up as much time as possible. The Steelers took more than seven minutes and 11 plays to march the length of the field. Franco Harris got the call again and again. Harris was on his way to a total of 158 rushing yards for the game, which was then a Super Bowl rushing record.

On the last play of the drive, with just three and a half minutes to play, Bradshaw threw a near-perfect four-yard pass to tight end Larry Brown in the end zone. Touchdown! The point-after was good, and the Steelers extended their lead to 10 points.

After the kickoff, the Steel Curtain slammed down on the Vikings. The game ended with the score 16-6; Pittsburgh captured its first NFL championship.

Franco Harris had played a remarkable game and was named the Most Valuable Player, but Terry Bradshaw had also played very well. The quarterback had completed nine of 14 passes for a total of 96 yards. Most importantly, he stood up to the tough Viking defense and threw one touchdown pass and no interceptions.

Terry Bradshaw's season-long comeback was now complete. He had returned from the side-lines to lead the Pittsburgh Steelers to victory in the Super Bowl, football's greatest achievement. No one would ever again question Terry Brad-shaw's abilities as a winning quarterback, in-cluding Bradshaw himself.

2

THE GROWTH OF A QUARTERBACK

Terry Bradshaw was born on September 2, 1948, in Shreveport, a small city in northern Louisiana. He was the second of three brothers.

Terry's father, Bill, was a hard-working man who had driven a truck before entering the navy. While stationed in Pensacola, Florida, he met a young woman, Novis, from Louisiana; they soon married. After leaving the military, Bill took a job with a manufacturing company, where he worked his way up over the years to a management position. Like many working-class families, the Bradshaws had little money and no luxuries, but Terry and his brothers had all the necessities of life while growing up.

Terry Bradshaw remembers his childhood as a very happy one. The best times were spent on his grandparents' farm in Louisiana, where Terry spent almost every summer of his youth.

Besides starring at quarterback in his senior year in high school, Bradshaw was also a national javelin champion.

The Bradshaws were a close and loving family. Their Baptist faith played an important role in their daily lives, and Terry's strong religious beliefs would always be a part of his life, even as an adult. While he was not above occasional mischief, Terry was an unusually well-behaved and obedient boy who gave his parents very little difficulty. Even as a teenager, he seldom found trouble or let it find him. The blond-haired, blue-eyed boy was handsome, with a warm friendly smile.

The Bradshaws moved to Iowa for a few years when Terry was young. Like many boys, he had a tremendous interest in sports. He enjoyed baseball and was the star pitcher on his Little League team. Football, however, was already his favorite sport. Even before he was able to throw a decent spiral pass, Terry decided he wanted to be a quarterback.

By the time the Bradshaw family returned to Shreveport—when Terry was 11 years old—football had taken over his life. If he was not playing the game, he was having a catch with his brother or a friend, or studying his form in a mirror, or tossing the ball against a wall and catching it himself. All his hopes and dreams concerned football, and in all his boyhood fantasies Terry pictured himself as a star quarterback.

Terry worked hard to develop his arm strength and accuracy, but it took some time for his talents to be recognized. He was left off his seventh-grade team and, after a summer of throwing drills and running, he was heartbroken when he was also not chosen for the eighth-grade team. But he hung around the team's practice field, hoping for a chance to show his abilities. One day, the coach saw him launch an accurate 50-yard throw when returning a stray football to the field where the team was practicing. The startled coach ran over to Bradshaw, and he immediately asked Terry to join the team. Terry quickly accepted.

Terry's best friend from eighth grade through college was Tommy Spinks, who was also a talented athlete and loved football as much as Bradshaw did. The two boys were inseparable and perfected their passing skills by playing catch almost every day.

Both Terry and Tommy dreamed of playing quarterback. By the time they began attending Woodlawn High School, each had the ability to throw strong, accurate passes. High school football was a very popular sport in northern Louisiana, and Woodlawn was one of the best teams in that part of the state. Both Bradshaw and Spinks made the school's football team. Until their senior year, the two close friends remained on the sidelines and waited for their chance to play, while the team's older quarterbacks led the offense.

Spinks was actually ranked above Bradshaw as a quarterback for the first three years of high school. He was a gifted all-around athlete, and Bradshaw convinced both his friend and Woodlawn's coach that Spinks's abilities would be more valuable to the team if he was used as a pass receiver. Spinks's move to receiver was a success. He turned out to have tremendous talent as a pass catcher and became the team's offensive star, setting several records in the process.

Terry Bradshaw became Woodlawn's starting quarterback, and he had a successful season; his well-thrown passes consistently found their way to Spinks and the other receivers. Although Bradshaw had had to wait until his senior year to become a starter, he demonstrated ability as a passer and offensive leader. He led Woodlawn to the final game of the tournament for state championship, which they lost 12-9.

Bradshaw's outstanding performance in the semi-final game of the championship tournament attracted the attention of college recruiters. Almost every college and university with a football team looks for big, strong-armed quarterbacks and dozens of schools contacted the Bradshaw family, hoping to entice Terry to accept a scholarship to their school.

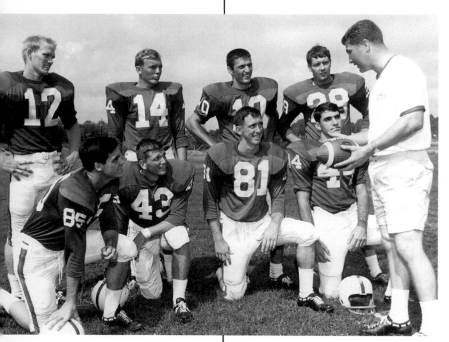

The freshman football team at Louisiana Tech included Bradshaw (number 12) and Tommy Spinks (number 43).

Bradshaw and his family narrowed the choice to three schools. Baylor University and Louisiana State University (LSU) in Baton Rouge were large universities with successful football programs. The third choice was Louisiana Tech University, a much smaller school located in Ruston, not far from Shreveport.

Baylor was eliminated from consideration after an unpleasant visit to the school. The young, somewhat naive Bradshaw was shocked and disappointed by the drinking, cigarette smoking, and wild behavior he observed among the football players he met there. He did not want to attend a college that condoned such conduct.

LSU soon became his first choice. It was a great honor to be recruited by such a prestigious football power, and the university very much wanted Bradshaw to attend. Playing football at LSU offered Bradshaw the chance to become a nationally known football star, which was still his dream.

After formally committing himself to attend LSU, however, Bradshaw had second thoughts. He realized that there would be a lot of pressure placed on him at the big school. If he started, he would be the linchpin in a major football program located in the state capital, and thousands of people would cheer for or against him every Saturday, all fall. The idea of playing in such a high-pressure situation made him very uncomfortable, as he seldom performed well in stressful conditions. He lacked the self-confidence needed to succeed at a big university like LSU, and he knew it would be a big mistake to attend the university.

Not knowing how to tell LSU, his family, and his friends that he had changed his mind, he deliberately did less than his best work on the entrance exam that was required by LSU. As a result, he failed the test.

Bradshaw accepted a scholarship offer from Louisiana Tech, whose smaller size and closeness to Shreveport were much to his liking. His brother Gary was already attending Louisiana Tech, and Tommy Spinks, as well as many of his friends, had also decided to attend the school. Bradshaw had made the right choice. "Louisiana Tech turned out to be perfect for me: small school, personal attention, small crowds, small-time schedule," Bradshaw recalled later. "It was just what I needed: a chance to play and mature."

In college, Bradshaw grew to a height of 6'3", which was tall for a quarterback at the time. He carried over 200 pounds on his rugged physique, which enabled him to survive the pounding that a quarterback must absorb from opposing defenses. He had good running ability which allowed him to evade pass rushers or run with the ball to pick up yardage when necessary. Most importantly, Bradshaw's throwing arm was unusually strong and accurate, and he was able to throw long "bombs" far down field to his receivers.

As a freshman, Bradshaw once again sat and watched, serving as the backup to an upperclassman quarterback. By the next season, Bradshaw was splitting the playing time with the other quarterback. The team seemed much improved with Bradshaw on the field, and he had some outstanding games.

Bradshaw was the starting quarterback as a junior, and he had a tremendous season. Bradshaw and Tommy Spinks proved once again to be a successful combination. The quarterback led his team to a 9-2 record and a victory in the Grantland Rice Bowl following the regular season; he was named the game's most valuable player. Bradshaw led all college players in total offensive yardage, a major accomplishment.

As a senior, Bradshaw had another solid season, although the team was less successful. Despite playing for a small university, Bradshaw's impressive college performance attracted the attention of the scouts for many NFL teams. He was recognized as one of best college players in the nation, and probably the most promising quarterback. Many experts believed that he had the ability to become a top-rank NFL quarterback.

One of Bradshaw's proudest accomplishments happened off the football field. Unlike many collegiate athletic stars, Bradshaw completed his academic work and graduated from college.

In the NFL's 1970 college draft, Terry Bradshaw was elated to be the first player selected, a tremendous honor. He was less happy, however, about joining the Pittsburgh Steelers, the NFL's worst team.

3
THE LONG ROAD TO SUCCESS

The Pittsburgh Steelers were one of the National Football League's oldest teams and, on the field, one of its least successful. The franchise had entered the league in 1933 and was still owned and run by its founder, Art Rooney, and his family. In all those years, the Steelers had never won an NFL championship. In recent seasons, their performance had been dismal, often finishing at the bottom of the league standings. Making matters worse, team management had consistently drafted college players who failed to develop into successful NFL players.

The situation began to change in 1969, when the Steelers hired Chuck Noll as their head coach. Formerly an assistant coach with the Baltimore Colts, the 37-year-old Noll was a brilliant and innovative strategist. Noll's team won its first game of the season, then dropped the remaining 13 games. Pittsburgh made progress, however, simply by ridding itself of unproduc-

Bradshaw had difficulty adjusting to the pro game and suffered a lack of confidence as a result.

tive veteran players and bringing in talented younger players, such as defensive end Joe Greene, the Steelers' first pick in the 1969 college draft.

Noll believed that strong defense won football games, and his efforts in his first season to improve the team's defensive unit were productive. The offense, however, was a disaster. The Steelers needed new talent at running back, receiver, and offensive lineman. Most of all, they needed a new quarterback. The Steelers' 1-13 record in 1969 earned them the first selection in the 1970 college draft. They used that pick to choose the quarterback most scouts agreed was the best available in the draft, Terry Bradshaw.

Terry Bradshaw and Jon Kolb (number 55) bring down Dick Butkus in a 1971 game against the Chicago Bears after Butkus intercepted a pass. The play was called back because of a penalty— but on the next play, Butkus again intercepted Bradshaw's pass.

Bradshaw's arrival in Pittsburgh was only one of the changes facing the Steelers that year. In 1970, following the merger of the NFL with the rival American Football League, the Steelers were grouped with two other NFL teams and all the AFL teams to form the new American Football Conference of the National Football League. The Steelers would now play most of their games against teams they had never faced before.

Terry Bradshaw, the 22-year-old rookie with the rifle arm and the friendly smile, was greeted by fans, sportswriters, new teammates, and coaches as the savior who would change the Steelers from NFL doormat to playoff contender. But despite his impressive physical abilities and his accomplishments on the field in college, Bradshaw was not ready to play in the NFL.

Playing quarterback at the NFL level required experience and knowledge that he could not get playing at a relatively small school such as Louisiana Tech. Big-time college football programs often use strategies and formations that resemble professional teams in complexity. At Louisiana Tech, Bradshaw had run only an uncomplicated offense against the very simple defensive schemes of the opposing teams. He had a lot to learn before he was ready to play effectively in the NFL.

On a personal level, Bradshaw was also not ready for the NFL. He had never lived very far from his family and friends, and had no experience with life in a big northern city such as Pittsburgh. He was open and friendly, a genuinely nice guy, but he was also insecure and nervous. "I came from a college that was not a major college program, and I came from a family that had sheltered me," Bradshaw later said. "I wasn't prepared for anything that was high pressure. I was extremely immature, I was extremely naive. I was not prepared for the NFL." Bradshaw's southern accent and tendency to speak slowly set him apart from many of his teammates and added to his discomfort.

Bradshaw's rookie season was difficult, with only a few bright moments on the field. While he connected with his receivers for six touchdowns, he also threw an unacceptable total of 24 interceptions. His nervousness in game conditions was obvious, and he made a lot of mistakes; but a lack of good running backs, receivers, and most importantly, offensive linemen added to Bradshaw's difficulties.

On most NFL teams, the coaching staff decided on the offensive play on the sidelines and told the quarterback what play to run. The Steelers, however, expected their quarterback to call his own play in the huddle and direct the offense on the field—a big responsibility. Bradshaw struggled with this duty. The young quarterback often seemed indecisive in huddles, changing his mind several times before finally deciding on a play. This annoyed some teammates and damaged their confidence in his leadership ability.

In his college career, Bradshaw had little experience with reading the defensive formations that he faced. Experienced quarterbacks know how to improvise when the play they have called starts to fall apart, or when the defense puts a lot of pressure on them. When Bradshaw was in that position, he looked like a dead duck. "As a rookie," Bradshaw would later comment, "I was totally lost."

In each of his first three games as a Steeler, Bradshaw had the unpleasant experience of being sacked in his own end zone for a safety. Rather than supporting their young quarterback, impatient Steeler fans booed his every mistake. Pittsburgh sportswriters were equally merciless, criticizing Bradshaw at every opportunity.

No one doubted Bradshaw's physical skills, but some critics began to question his intelligence. He did not seem to be learning from his mistakes. Because of his struggles to adjust to life in the NFL, Bradshaw earned the unfair reputation of being a dummy, a label that stuck with him for a long time.

In Bradshaw's rookie season, the Steelers were an improved team due largely to their defense, which was becoming one of the best in the league. The team enjoyed its best season in

The Steel Curtain was perhaps the greatest group of defensive linemen ever to play the game. From left to right: L. C. Greenwood, Ernie Holmes, "Mean" Joe Greene, and Dwight White.

many years; after eight games, they had won four and lost four—a remarkable comeback after winning only one game the previous season. But the Steelers lost five of their last six games to finish at 5-9.

After the season, Bradshaw returned home to Louisiana, where he would continue to live between football seasons. He married Melissa Babich, a former Miss Teenage America, whom he had known since his days at Louisiana Tech. The marriage was a mistake, and Bradshaw takes the blame for its failure "because I was too immature to own up to my true feelings." The couple separated after less than a year and were later divorced.

The Steelers again improved in 1971, winning six games while losing eight. The defensive unit remained the strongest part of the team, anchored by "Mean" Joe Greene at defensive end. Defensive ends L. C. Greenwood and Dwight White, linebacker Jack Ham, and defensive backs Mel Blount and Glen Edwards had joined the team and quickly made big contributions to the Steelers' efforts. On offense, running backs Frenchy Fuqua and Preston Pearson and wide receiver Ron Shanklin all had solid seasons. Bradshaw played with greater consistency as well. He threw 13 touchdown passes and completed 54 percent of his passes. Interceptions remained a problem, but Bradshaw showed significant progress in his development as an NFL quarterback. The Steelers finished the season in second place in the AFC Central Division, an encouraging advancement for the young team.

The arrival of talented running back Franco Harris in 1972 was a big step in the emergence of the Pittsburgh Steelers as a winning team. The powerful rusher combined strength, speed, and elusiveness, and quickly became the backbone of the Steelers' offense. Harris's contributions took a lot of pressure off Bradshaw, who was no longer expected to carry the majority of the offensive burden.

The Steelers had a tremendous 1972 season. The defensive unit, now nicknamed the Steel Curtain, overpowered the opposition all year long. Harris rushed for 1,055 yards and 10 touchdowns. Bradshaw threw 12 touchdown passes while also rushing for seven scores.

On several occasions, Bradshaw displayed great courage in leading comebacks that resulted in Pittsburgh victories. These gutsy performances made Bradshaw a hero to many of the Steelers fans and also earned him the re-spect of his teammates. While he still threw too many interceptions and made other mental er-rors, the mistakes happened less frequently.

The Steelers posted an 11-3 record and won the Central Division title, thereby qualifying for the playoffs for the first time since the merger with the AFL. Their opponent in their first playoff game was the Oakland Raiders, always one of the league's best teams.

Before an enthusiastic crowd in a sold-out Three Rivers Stadium, the Steel Curtain shut down the powerful Raiders offense, and Oakland responded by nearly shutting down Franco Har-ris's attempts to run. Nevertheless, Bradshaw got his team close enough to kick two field goals, and Pittsburgh took a 6-0 lead into the fourth quarter. With less than four minutes left to play, Raider quarterback Ken Stabler took advantage of a Steeler safety blitz and threw a touchdown pass that gave his team the lead. With 72 sec-onds left in the game and the ball on the Pitts-burgh 40 yardline, Bradshaw was down to his last chance. He had thrown three straight in-completions, and if he could not gain a first down, the Raiders would get the ball back, and the game would essentially be over.

Bradshaw took the snap and "felt the heat of the Raider rush like a blowtorch," he later wrote. Downfield, Frenchy Fuqua was open over the middle. Bradshaw zipped the pass a split second before a Raider defenseman put him on the ground.

Lying on his back, Bradshaw heard the roar of the crowd, but he could not know for sure what had happened. As it turns out, even on re-play, it is difficult to tell exactly what happened.

The ball bounced off someone—perhaps Frenchy Fuqua, or perhaps a Raider defender—and caromed into the arms of Franco Harris, who caught it and ran into the end zone.

The referee refused to signal a touchdown. If Fuqua had touched the ball first, according to the rules at the time, the touchdown would not be allowed. The referee went over to the sidelines and watched a replay on a special TV, even though the rules officially did not allow this. After watching the play several times, the referee decided he could not tell who had touched the ball before Harris caught it, and ruled in favor of Pittsburgh. The "Immaculate Reception," as the play later came to be known, gave the Steelers a 13-7 victory, and Bradshaw his first taste of real success and fame. Steelers' fans felt as if they had seen the future.

Franco Harris was mobbed by ecstatic fans moments after catching the "Immaculate Reception" in 1972.

The Steelers met the Miami Dolphins the following Sunday in the AFC Championship Game. Bradshaw's performance had both high and low points. In the first quarter, he fumbled at the Miami 3 yardline. Luckily, a teammate pounced on the ball in the end zone, resulting in a Pittsburgh touchdown. Bradshaw, however, was hit hard on the play and left the game complaining of dizziness.

The quarterback returned to the game in the

fourth quarter with seven minutes to play and Pittsburgh trailing 21-10. He led his team downfield and threw a touchdown pass to wide receiver Al Young. But on Pittsburgh's final two possessions, Bradshaw threw interceptions that ended their hopes of a comeback. Miami won, 21-17, and went on to defeat the Washington Redskins in the Super Bowl two weeks later.

The loss was a disappointing conclusion to an otherwise outstanding season. A team is always happy when a little luck comes their way, as in the Immaculate Reception. But having talent and playing hard are the most important things, and the Steelers and Terry Bradshaw were about to prove that true again and again.

Despite his early struggles, Terry Bradshaw had earned the respect of his teammates and the Steelers' fans by 1973. He had proven his importance to the team and was considered as essential to their success as Franco Harris or the Steel Curtain. One person remained unconvinced, though, and that was Coach Chuck Noll. Bradshaw had shown slow but steady improvement, but his inconsistency continued to bother Noll, who believed that the problem was Bradshaw's preparation and attitude.

Bradshaw loved to play the game; but he admits that early in his career his preparation between games was less than adequate, a fact that did not escape Noll's attention. A successful quarterback works hard both on and off the field. The long hours of off-field study—watching game films and studying the playbook—were very boring and the part of being a quarterback

Chuck Noll shows his displeasure over a mistake by Bradshaw. As the seasons wore on, however, Bradshaw developed into an expert quarterback.

that Bradshaw liked least.

Noll also thought that Bradshaw approached the game with less intensity than was necessary. A quarterback must always be in control of both himself and his team, and it requires a high level of concentration and awareness. Noll felt that this type of mental focus was often missing in Bradshaw. When Noll screamed at his young quarterback on the sidelines in the middle of games it was to get him to concentrate on the situation and focus on what he needed to do.

While Bradshaw was disturbed by the rough treatment he received from Noll, he later came to understand what his coach was trying to do. "Chuck knew I had gotten by on pure talent all of my football career and one day I was going to need more than that in the NFL if I was going to be successful. I had to know how to use my ability. Eventually I found out Chuck was right."

Bradshaw summed up their relationship by stating that "Chuck Noll was right in the way he handled me, because it made me a better quarterback."

The Steelers' 1973 season was very frustrating. Although the team played well and tied the Cincinnati Bengals for best record in the AFC's Central Division, injuries plagued them all season long. Franco Harris and Frenchy Fuqua both missed a number of games. Bradshaw played well until he suffered a shoulder separation that knocked him out of the lineup at midseason. Bradshaw's backup, Terry Hanratty, stepped in for several games before he, too, was injured. Rookie Joe Gilliam took over briefly before Bradshaw's shoulder healed sufficiently for him to

Bradshaw winces in pain after breaking his collarbone on a keeper play in 1973.

reclaim the quarterback job. His shoulder still bothered him, though, and he threw seven interceptions in Pittsburgh's last two regular season games.

The Steelers faced the Oakland Raiders again in the 1973 playoffs, and the game was a struggle for Pittsburgh from the opening kick. By the end of the third quarter the Raiders led 23-7, and Bradshaw crippled Pittsburgh's chances for victory by throwing three crucial interceptions. The game ended with the score Oakland 33, Pittsburgh 14.

By the beginning of the following season, Terry Bradshaw's life was in turmoil both on and off the football field. Chuck Noll had decided to let Bradshaw compete with both Terry Hanratty and Joe Gilliam for the starting job that had been Bradshaw's for the previous four seasons. Much to the disappointment of the young man from Louisiana, Noll named the promising but inexperienced Gilliam as the starter before the first game of the regular season. Bradshaw was hurt and embarrassed by the decision.

With this setback in his career, Bradshaw was at the lowest point he had ever known in his life. His life seemed without purpose, and he was utterly miserable. He was terrified that his football career might be ending.

Helped greatly by his strong religious beliefs, Bradshaw survived the ordeal. For six weeks, he waited his turn on the sidelines and did what he could to support Gilliam and the offense. He demonstrated a remarkably positive attitude under difficult circumstances.

Steeler running back Rocky Bleier knew how Bradshaw felt about the demotion: "Bradshaw performed his sideline duty with a false show of indifference. He tried to cover his disappointment with a big, wide smile. In reality, though, it was killing him."

Gilliam played adequately at best, and Bradshaw replaced him at quarterback late in the game on several occasions. In these situations, Bradshaw played well enough to regain the starting job in the second half of the season. Bleier noticed a tremendous change in Bradshaw when he returned to the lineup. "His presence in the lineup was dramatically different. And in the locker room, he was suddenly friendlier, more down-to-earth, feeling less pressured to do it all himself."

Grateful for a second chance to prove himself and eager to show he deserved the opportunity, Bradshaw played as well as he ever had. He consistently demonstrated the concentration and leadership that had sometimes been missing in the past.

Rookie wide receivers Lynn Swann and John Stallworth, who joined the Steelers at the beginning of the 1974 season, were major additions to the Pittsburgh offense. Both were blessed with great speed and excellent hands, and were the ideal targets for Bradshaw's long-distance bombs. With top-notch receivers and better pass blocking, the Steelers' offensive unit was much improved.

The defense was more awesome than ever, adding middle linebacker Jack Lambert and safety Donnie Shell to their already powerful lineup. The Steel Curtain overwhelmed opposing offenses all season long and was the major reason why the Steelers captured their third consecutive AFC Central Division title.

Pittsburgh easily defeated the Buffalo Bills

in their first playoff game, and they avenged their loss to the Raiders a year earlier with a thrilling, come-from-behind victory in which Bradshaw led his teammates to three fourth-quarter touchdowns and a 24-13 win.

The impressive 16-6 victory over Minnesota in Super Bowl IX demonstrated how great a team the Steelers had become. The Vikings under Coach Bud Grant were making their third Super Bowl appearance in four years, and the nucleus of the team was so strong that they would be back yet again two years later. But the Steel Curtain allowed no points to the strong Viking offense, with Minnesota's defense scoring their only points on a recovered fumble. Bradshaw and the offensive unit put on an im-

John Stallworth was one of the most dependable wide receivers in the game. Along with Lynn Swann, the duo was known to their fellow Steelers as the "China Dolls" because they were not supposed to be hit hard in practice.

pressive demonstration of "ball control" football, with Franco Harris providing most of the heroics with his 158-yard rushing performance.

Although Bradshaw's contributions were less obvious than those of his big running back, he engineered the two scoring drives that captured the victory for the Steelers, calling the right plays at the right time to overcome the strong effort of the Minnesota defense. After 42 seasons of frustration in Pittsburgh, Terry Bradshaw and his teammates had led the Steelers to their first NFL Championship.

To his players, Chuck Noll had stressed hard work and determination as essential elements in the team's success. No player was more important than the good of the team, and there were no ego problems on the Steelers. Everybody on the team contributed to the effort, and therefore everyone was a significant part of the team. The Steelers' strong work ethic appealed to many football fans throughout the country, and nowhere were they more appreciated than in the largely blue-collar, working-class city of Pittsburgh.

After enduring the long, five-year climb from mediocrity to world champions, Terry Bradshaw should have been overjoyed by the Steelers' Super Bowl victory. Actually, he had very mixed feelings.

It had been an extremely difficult year for Bradshaw. Joe Gilliam had been the Steeler quarterback for half of the season, and Bradshaw believed that Gilliam deserved a large part of the credit for the team's success. "I didn't feel I could celebrate with my teammates because I hadn't completely earned it. I felt I had only been a piece of the puzzle."

Bradshaw returned to his ranch in Louisiana to reflect on the remarkable season that had just ended. Confident that he could improve on his performance, Bradshaw was determined to raise his game to a higher level the following season.

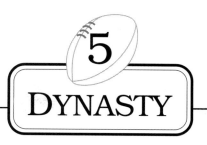

5
DYNASTY

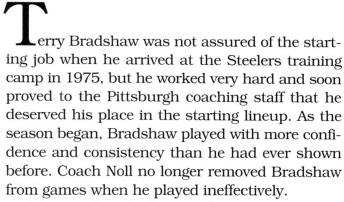

Terry Bradshaw was not assured of the starting job when he arrived at the Steelers training camp in 1975, but he worked very hard and soon proved to the Pittsburgh coaching staff that he deserved his place in the starting lineup. As the season began, Bradshaw played with more confidence and consistency than he had ever shown before. Coach Noll no longer removed Bradshaw from games when he played ineffectively.

The Steelers had a terrific regular season, winning 12 games while losing only two. After an easy win over the Baltimore Colts in their first playoff game, they met the Raiders again for the AFC Championship. The game remained a defensive struggle for three quarters, with Pittsburgh holding a 3-0 lead.

Finally, in the fourth quarter, Franco Harris rushed for one touchdown, and Bradshaw hit Stallworth on a 20-yard pass that resulted in

Terry Bradshaw releases the ball just before being leveled by Ed "Too Tall" Jones in the 1976 Super Bowl against the Dallas Cowboys.

another six points (the point-after attempt was unsuccessful). Oakland quarterback Ken Stabler answered back with a touchdown pass to Mike Siani, and the Raiders' 48-year-old kicker, George Blanda, added a field goal for another three points. Oakland got the ball back and had one more chance to score, but the Steeler defense held, and Pittsburgh won the game by a margin of 16-10.

On January 18, 1976, the Steelers met the Dallas Cowboys in Miami, Florida, in Super Bowl X. Dallas had had a surprisingly successful season for a team made up largely of aging veterans and untested rookies.

Each team scored a touchdown in the opening quarter, with Roger Staubach, the Cowboys' quarterback, finding receiver Drew Pearson on a 29-yard scoring pass four and a half minutes into the game. The Steelers answered back three minutes later, as Bradshaw threw a touchdown pass to tight end Randy Grossman.

The defenses then took charge of the game, and for the next two quarters, neither team could reach the end zone. The only score was a second-quarter Dallas field goal. At the beginning of the fourth quarter, Reggie Harrison blocked a Dallas punt—the kick hit him in the helmet. The ball bounced through the end zone and out of bounds, resulting in a Pittsburgh safety. Dallas' lead was reduced to 10-9, until Roy Gerela booted two field goals to give the Steelers a 15-10 lead.

With three and a half minutes to go, the outcome of the game was still very much in doubt. After calling two running plays that picked up six yards, Bradshaw faced a third down and four

Lynn Swann was named the Most Valuable Player in Super Bowl X after making sensational catches like this one against the Cowboys' Mark Washington. He ended the game with a record 161 receiving yards.

yards to go on the Pittsburgh 36 yardline. In the huddle, Lynn Swann announced that he thought that he could get open downfield. Swann had already caught three passes for a total of 97 yards. Bradshaw told him that he would look for him deep.

As Swann took off down the middle of the field, Bradshaw recognized Dallas' blitz formation and knew that he had only a few seconds at best to throw the ball before he was tackled. He held the ball as long as he could in order to give Swann time to get open. Then, just as Cowboy

Linebacker Jack Lambert was the personification of the Pittsburgh Steelers' blue collar, in-your-face mentality.

safety Cliff Harris was about to level him, Bradshaw reached back and threw a long bomb. The ball, tightly spiralling, hurtled in a perfect arc and traveled 59 yards right into Swann's waiting hands. The receiver ran five yards into the end zone. Touchdown!

Harris's hit knocked Bradshaw unconscious. He was revived quickly, but had to be helped to the sidelines, his legs still wobbly. It was one of the most exciting plays in Super Bowl history. Gerela missed the extra point, so Pittsburgh now held a 21-10 lead with three minutes left on the game clock.

Dallas got the ball back, and Staubach led his team rapidly down the field for a touchdown. With Terry Hanratty replacing Bradshaw at quarterback, the Steelers were unable to pick up a first down, and Dallas had another chance. Staubach was famous for leading last-second comebacks, but the Steel Curtain performed its usual heroics. Pittsburgh captured its second consecutive Super Bowl, 21-17.

Lynn Swann, who had caught four passes for 161 yards and a touchdown, was named the game's most valuable player. Bradshaw earned praise for his gutsy performance. He was in no mood to celebrate immediately following the game. He had suffered a concussion, a head injury that potentially can be very serious. Still groggy, Bradshaw was being treated by the medical staff in the Pittsburgh locker room as his teammates were celebrating nearby.

After the best season of his career, Bradshaw headed home to Louisiana to recuperate. Although he had been selected to play in the Pro Bowl, the NFL's post-season all-star game, he had to miss the game because of the concussion.

The 1976 season was disappointing for the Steelers. They lost four of their first five games and suffered a series of injuries to key players. Bradshaw himself was injured twice and missed a total of four games. Still, there were bright spots for Pittsburgh. Middle linebacker Jack Lambert emerged as one of the NFL's best defensive players, and Franco Harris and veteran Rocky Bleier each rushed for over 1,000 yards, a rare accomplishment. Fighting injuries much of the year, Bradshaw had a good season, but he was not as productive as the previous campaign.

Oakland finally earned its revenge on the Steelers in the 1976 AFC Championship Game, defeating them 24-7. Harris and Bleier both missed the game due to injuries. Oakland went on to win its first NFL Championship in Super Bowl XI two weeks later.

The 1977 season was also a disappointment for Bradshaw and the Steelers, and they could not blame their mediocre performance on injuries. The Steelers simply did not play well, although they managed to capture the Central Division title among weak competition with a record of 9-5. The Denver Broncos knocked Pittsburgh out of the playoffs in the first round. Bradshaw threw for a touchdown and ran for another, but he also tossed three interceptions as Pittsburgh was defeated 34-21.

After two disappointing seasons, many people wondered whether the Pittsburgh Steelers were finished as one of the NFL's dominant teams. It was said that they were too old to repeat their previous triumphs.

6

BACK ON TOP

In 1978, the Pittsburgh Steelers played so well that the two previous seasons seemed like a bad dream. During the regular season, they posted a 14-2 record, the best in the league. They played unusually aggressive and intelligent football, and their superb performance earned them their sixth AFC Central Division title in seven years.

At the age of 30 and in his ninth year in the NFL, Terry Bradshaw enjoyed his finest season. Using the NFL's complicated system for rating the efficiency of its quarterbacks, Bradshaw was rated the AFC's best in 1978. As a result of his outstanding performance, Bradshaw was named the NFL's most valuable player. He was also voted the starting quarterback in the Pro Bowl game for the first time.

In the playoffs, the Steelers easily defeated the Denver Broncos 33-10 at Three Rivers Stadium, as Bradshaw connected with both Swann

Back on top. Bradshaw celebrates after leading the Steelers to their third Super Bowl win, in 1979.

and Stallworth on touchdown passes. In their next playoff contest, Pittsburgh demolished the Houston Oilers. The Steel Curtain held rookie Earl Campbell, the league's leading rusher, to just 62 yards on the ground. They also intercepted five Dan Pastorini passes. Despite the weather, Bradshaw again had touchdown throws to both Stallworth and Swann. The game was so one-sided that it was basically decided by half time, with Pittsburgh leading 31-3. They eventually won the game 34-5.

Super Bowl XIII, played in Miami on January 21, 1979, once again pitted the Steelers against the Dallas Cowboys. In the first quarter, each team had a fumble that was recovered by the other team, and both turnovers resulted in touchdowns. Dallas scored again in the second quarter on a Bradshaw fumble, his second of the game. Dallas now led 14-7.

Deep in Pittsburgh territory, Bradshaw found John Stallworth on a short pass just 10 yards beyond the line of scrimmage. After catching the ball, Stallworth broke free of an attempted tackle by the Cowboys' Aaron Kyle and streaked the length of the field for a touchdown, his second of the contest. Then Pittsburgh cornerback Mel Blount intercepted a Roger Staubach pass with about a minute left in the first half, and Bradshaw threw a short touchdown pass to running back Rocky Bleier for another Pittsburgh score. At the halftime break, the score was Pittsburgh 21, Dallas 14.

The only scoring in the third quarter was a Dallas field goal. The fourth quarter began with the Steeler offense driving the ball downfield. Franco Harris burst through a big hole at the line of scrimmage to run 22 yards for another Pittsburgh touchdown. Another Dallas fumble let Bradshaw throw an 18-yard strike to Lynn Swann for Pittsburgh's final points. A heroic Roger Staubach led the Cowboys to two late touchdowns, but time ran out on the Dallas comeback. The final score was Pittsburgh 35, Dallas 31.

Terry Bradshaw finished with 318 yards passing and four touchdowns, which was then a Super Bowl record. The Pittsburgh quarterback was named the game's most valuable player. Bradshaw viewed his performance in Super Bowl XIV as the greatest achievement of his career.

In 1977, Bradshaw married Jo Jo Starbuck, a star of the Ice Capades. The popular skating show travelled and performed around the world for most of the year; as a result, the couple rarely got to see each other. Differences soon developed between them. By the time the Steelers began their 1979 season, Terry Bradshaw's second marriage was already in serious trouble. Jo Jo Starbuck filed for divorce in August 1980.

Bradshaw's marital problems left him heartbroken and depressed. However, he refused to allow the unhappiness in his personal life to interfere with his performance on the football field. His 1979 season approached the high standards he had set the previous year as he threw for 26 touchdowns and 3,724 passing yards, the highest total of his career.

The Steelers had another solid season. They did not dominate their opponents as they had in 1978, but they did post an excellent 12-4 record and another Central Division title. Convincing

Jo Jo Starbuck had competed in the Winter Olympics in the pair figure-skating competition before marrying Terry Bradshaw in 1977.

Despite the injuries he had sustained, Bradshaw could still run and throw after 10 years in the NFL. He had finally lived up to all the expectations and hopes the Steelers had when they drafted him.

victories at Three Rivers Stadium over Miami and Houston sent the Steelers to the Super Bowl for the fourth time.

Super Bowl XIV was played on January 20, 1980, in Pasadena, California, only a short distance from the home field of the Los Angeles Rams, the NFC champs. The Rams had qualified for the playoffs with a record of just 9-7, the worst record ever of any team to make it to the Super Bowl. The Cinderella team had overcome a number of injuries, including those to their starting quarterback. The inexperienced Vince Ferragamo was the Rams' quarterback for the Super Bowl.

Los Angeles played a strong and courageous game. After three quarters they led the Steelers by a score of 19-17. Bradshaw had thrown a touchdown pass to Lynn Swann early in the second half, but he had also thrown three interceptions.

In the fourth quarter, Bradshaw threw a long bomb to John Stallworth, who scored a touchdown, and Pittsburgh took a 24-19 lead. Los Angeles began a long drive of their own, but Steeler middle linebacker Jack Lambert intercepted a Ferragamo pass, ending the Rams' threat. Bradshaw and the Pittsburgh offense took over and moved slowly and steadily 70 yards down the field. Franco Harris dove over his blockers and into the end zone for the final Pittsburgh touchdown. The final score was Pittsburgh 31, Los Angeles 19.

The Steelers had won their fourth Super Bowl, a remarkable achievement, and they had accomplished this feat in just six seasons. The San Francisco 49ers equalled this record of four Super Bowl victories in the 1980s, but they did it over nine seasons. Chuck Noll became the only coach in NFL history to guide his team to four championships.

Bradshaw was named the Super Bowl's most valuable player for the second consecutive season, an honor he felt was not deserved. He had thrown for 309 yards and two touchdowns, but he had also thrown three interceptions. Bradshaw believed that both Stallworth and Swann were more deserving of the MVP Award.

In 1980, injuries struck many key offensive players, including John Stallworth, Lynn Swann, Franco Harris, and Bradshaw, who missed several games. The Steel Curtain defense had aged and could no longer overpower all the opposition.

Many of the best players on the Steelers were now 30 years old or more, and they were physically no longer capable of performing at the level of previous seasons. The team also seemed to play with less emotional intensity, as if winning was no longer as important. The result was a disappointing season. The Steelers finished with a mediocre 9-7 record and missed the playoffs for the first time since 1973.

After an amazing run of success, the Pittsburgh Steelers dynasty was coming to an end. At 32 years of age and recovering from a painful divorce, Terry Bradshaw began to give more consideration to his life outside football.

7

AFTER THE GAME

Despite a rapidly thinning hairline, Bradshaw was a handsome man with a sense of humor and an outgoing personality. He received many offers from the entertainment world and was intrigued enough to give show business a try.

In his first foray into acting, he appeared in small roles in two popular comedies starring Burt Reynolds in the late 1970s. He also pursued a brief singing career, recording a country and western album and touring with his own band. This adventure failed miserably and cost Bradshaw a lot of money.

After the Steelers' disappointing 1980 season, Bradshaw received an offer to star in his own television series, a comedy based on the world of stock car racing. He filmed a pilot episode of the show and was very enthusiastic about this opportunity. He told reporters that if

With an icepack on his arm, Bradshaw confers with backup quarterback Cliff Stoudt upon returning to action against the New York Jets in 1983.

"Stockers" was picked up as a weekly show, he was ready to retire from football.

The first episode of "Stockers" was shown once and very poorly received. No network offered to pick the series up, and Bradshaw returned to the Steelers for the 1981 season. His plans for an acting career and discussion of retirement, however, had angered Coach Noll, who questioned the quarterback's dedication to the team. As a result, Bradshaw's relationship with Noll, which had improved during their years of success, was badly damaged. The quarterback and his coach now barely spoke to one another.

An aging Pittsburgh Steelers team struggled in 1981. They played well for short stretches but lost their last two games of the season after Bradshaw suffered a broken bone in his hand. Rookie backup quarterback Mark Malone was unable to rally the team, and they missed the playoffs with a record of 8-8, their worst season in a decade. Until his injury, Bradshaw was having a solid season, completing 54 percent of his passes, with 22 touchdowns and only 14 interceptions. Although the Steelers were past their peak as a team, Bradshaw's 1981 performance was among his finest.

Football is a violent sport, and injuries are a frequent occurrence. Every NFL player learns to play while experiencing pain; it is part of the game, despite the risk of permanent injury. Bradshaw had been hurt many times but had usually continued to play unless the injury was a serious one, such as a broken bone or a separation. Before the 1982 season, though, at the age of 34, Bradshaw suffered an injury that proved to be the most serious of his career.

In training camp, Bradshaw threw a pass and suddenly felt a sharp pain in his elbow. The pain did not go away over the next few days, and Bradshaw continued to play, despite the fact that his elbow hurt every time he threw the ball. When the regular season began, he started receiving pain-killing injections that lessened his discomfort. Continuing to play did not allow the elbow to heal, though, and his arm still hurt every time he threw a pass. A 57-day strike by the NFL Players Union gave Bradshaw some much-needed rest, but the pain was still there when the strike ended.

Despite his elbow injury, Bradshaw had another productive season. There were a number of new faces on the team, but the Steelers played well enough to make the playoffs for the first time in three years.

They met the San Diego Chargers, who had one of the AFC's most dangerous offenses. Bradshaw threw for one touchdown, ran for another, and completed 28 of 39 passes for 325 yards. But the Steelers' defense could not stop

As an actor, Bradshaw never could do much more than tread water. Here he is in a scene from The Cannonball Run *with country music star Mel Tillis. Burt Reynolds, Roger Moore, Farrah Fawcett, and Dom DeLuise had bigger roles in this movie.*

Bradshaw's last professional game was a winner. Playing despite great pain, he threw two touchdown passes as the Steelers earned another play-off berth in 1983.

the Chargers, and Pittsburgh lost 31-28.

Bradshaw had surgery on his damaged elbow after the season and was still recuperating from the operation when the 1983 season began. The Steelers were unhappy that Bradshaw was unable to play, but the veteran quarterback would not return until he felt his elbow had entirely healed. He did not want to risk permanent damage to his throwing arm.

The Steelers asked him to stay away from practices and games until he was ready to play. He was hurt by this request, as he was by Noll's statement to the press that he should retire if he could not play. Still, Bradshaw continued to work regularly with rehabilitation equipment to strengthen his elbow so that he could return and help his team.

Finally, the arm began to respond to the treatment. With the Steelers having lost three straight games and fighting for a play-off berth, Bradshaw was activated for the last game of the season against the New York Jets.

While practicing two days before the game against the Jets, Bradshaw again felt pain in his elbow. He recalled, "My elbow was killing me and I was scared to death. Absolutely distraught. I didn't know what to do."

Despite the excruciating pain and months of inactivity, Bradshaw was in the starting lineup against the Jets. In one of the most heroic games of his career, Bradshaw led the Steelers down the field in the first quarter and threw a pass to wide receiver Gregg Garrity, who scored a touchdown. As he threw the pass, his elbow exploded with pain, and Bradshaw knew he had caused more damage to his injured arm. Still, for the good of his team, he decided to try to remain in the game.

The Steelers got the ball back, and Bradshaw engineered another long and successful drive towards the Jets' end zone. He threw a wobbly pass which Calvin Sweeney caught for a touchdown. It was the last pass he would throw in a pro game. The Steelers led 14-0 and went on to win 34-7, qualifying for the playoffs. But the veteran quarterback watched the rest of the game in excruciating pain.

Rather than have another operation, Bradshaw rested his arm for several months, and the elbow felt better. But when he tried to throw at the Steelers' May mini-camp, he once again felt sharp pain in his elbow. He decided right then that he would retire. He informed Chuck Noll of his decision, then went home and cried.

It had been a remarkable career. In 14 seasons Bradshaw had led the Steelers to the playoffs nine times and to the Super Bowl four times. He had completed 2,025 passes, 212 for touchdowns, and gained 27,989 yards passing.

After Bradshaw's retirement, Chuck Noll and the Pittsburgh Steelers went through a number of quarterbacks, none of whom were able to provide the type of leadership that Bradshaw had brought to the team. Most seasons the Steelers did not even qualify for the playoffs. Noll retired after the 1991 season, never reaching a Super Bowl without Terry Bradshaw as his quarterback.

Bradshaw had no intention of spending the remainder of his life at leisure. Soon after his retirement announcement, he accepted an offer from CBS Sports to become a game analyst for the network's football telecasts. He struggled at first and received much negative criticism. Many viewers felt that he talked too much, and he sounded nervous and awkward.

Bradshaw soon overcame his early difficulties. He worked very hard to learn his new job, and his broadcasting style improved rapidly. The years that he had spent running the Steelers' offense provided him with tremendous football knowledge. He demonstrated that he was very capable of sharing his knowledge of the sport with television viewers.

In 1985, Terry Bradshaw married for the third time. His marriage to Charla Hopkins, whom he had known for four years, provided him with the love and happiness that been missing for much of his life. The couple settled into a happy and fulfilling life on Bradshaw's Louisiana ranch. They have two children.

In 1989, Terry Bradshaw was awarded one of football's greatest honors when he was elected to the Pro Football Hall of Fame. Mel Blount, his Steeler teammate, was elected the same year. By 1994, eight members of the great Steelers organization of the Super Bowl years had been inducted into the Hall of Fame, including coach Chuck Noll and owner Art Rooney. It seems likely that other members of the Steelers' great championship teams will join them someday.

Few quarterbacks have equalled the high standards of production and leadership that Bradshaw brought to the Pittsburgh Steelers. He overcame major obstacles early in his career to lead his team to four Super Bowl victories in just six seasons, a record that may never be surpassed. More than 10 years after his retirement from football, Terry Bradshaw remains one of the sport's greatest champions.

TERRY BRADSHAW:
A CHRONOLOGY

1948   Terry Bradshaw born in Shreveport, Louisiana

1965   Quarterbacks high school team to state championship game

1966   Enrolls at Louisiana Tech University

1968   Becomes LTU's starting quarterback; leads team to 9-2 record and a bowl game victory; leads all college players in total offensive yardage

1970   Bradshaw is first player selected in the annual college draft by the Pittsburgh Steelers; becomes Steelers' starting quarterback but struggles in his rookie season

1972   Leads Steelers to AFC Central Division title and first playoff appearance, including stunning last-minute victory against Oakland Raiders, before losing to Miami Dolphins in second round

1974   After being benched early in season, returns to lead Steelers to Central Division championship and playoffs

1975   Pittsburgh defeats the Minnesota Vikings in Super Bowl IX; Bradshaw helps Steelers capture another Central Division title

1976   Pittsburgh wins Super Bowl X against the Dallas Cowboys

1978   Bradshaw has his best season in the NFL and is selected to the NFL Pro Bowl

1979   Steelers defeat Dallas Cowboys in Super Bowl XII; Bradshaw again selected to Pro Bowl

1980   Steelers defeat Los Angeles Rams in Super Bowl XIV

1983   Suffers serious injury to throwing arm during preseason; returns in last game of the season to throw two critical touchdown passes versus the New York Jets, enabling Steelers to clinch playoff berth; reinjures arm

1984   Retires from football. Begins second career as football commentator for CBS television

1989   Elected to Pro Football Hall of Fame

1994   Hired by Fox television as football commentator

STATISTICS

TERRY BRADSHAW
Pittsburgh Steelers

YEAR	G	PASSING ATT	CMP	PCT	GAIN	TD	INT	RUSHING ATT	YDS	AVG	TD
1970	13	218	83	38.1	1410	6	24	32	233	7.3	1
1971	14	373	203	54.4	2259	13	22	53	247	4.7	5
1972	14	308	147	47.7	1887	12	12	58	346	6.0	7
1973	10	180	89	49.4	1183	10	15	34	145	4.3	3
1974	8	148	67	45.3	785	7	8	34	224	6.6	2
1975	14	286	165	57.7	2055	18	9	35	210	6.0	3
1976	10	192	92	47.9	1177	10	9	31	219	7.1	3
1977	14	314	162	51.6	2523	17	19	31	171	5.5	3
1978	16	368	207	56.3	2915	28	20	32	93	2.9	1
1979	16	472	259	54.9	3724	26	25	21	83	4.0	0
1980	15	424	218	51.4	3339	24	22	36	111	3.1	2
1981	14	370	201	54.3	2887	22	14	38	162	4.3	2
1982	9	240	127	52.9	1768	17	11	8	10	1.3	0
1983	1	8	5	62.5	77	2	0	1	3	3.0	0
TOTALS	168	3901	2025	51.9	27989	212	210	444	2257	5.1	32

ATT   attempts
CMP   completions
GAIN   yards gained
TD   touchdowns
INT   interceptions

SUGGESTIONS FOR FURTHER READING

Bleier, Rocky, with Terry O'Neil. *Fighting Back.* Stein & Day: New York 1975.

Bradshaw, Terry, with Buddy Martin. *Looking Deep.* Contemporary Books: New York 1989.

Herskowitz, Mickey. *The Quarterbacks.* William Morrow and Company: New York 1990.

Neft, David S., Richard M. Cohen and Rick Korch. *Sports Encyclopedia: Pro Football, The.* St. Martin's Press: New York 1993.

Official National Football League 1993 Record & Fact Book, The, Workman Publishing: New York 1993.

Dienhart, Tom, Joe Hoppel, and Dave Sloan, editors. *The Sporting News Complete Super Bowl Book,* 1993 Edition. The Sporting News Publishing Company: St. Louis 1993.

ABOUT THE AUTHOR

Ron Frankl is a graduate of Haverford College. He is the author of *Duke Ellington* and *Charlie Parker* for Chelsea House Publishers' "Black Americans of Achievement" series, *Bruce Springsteen* for the "Popular Culture Legends" series, and *Wilt Chamberlain* for the "Basketball Legends" series.

INDEX

PICTURE CREDITS
UPI/Bettmann Newsphotos: pp. 2, 10, 13, 26, 32, 36, 42, 45, 48, 51, 54, 58; AP/Wide World Photos: pp. 8, 52; Courtesy LSU-Shreveport Archives: p. 16; Louisiana Tech University, Sports Information Office: p. 20; Courtesy Pittsburgh Steelers: pp. 24, 29, 34, 39, 46.

'Til All the Stars

Have Fallen

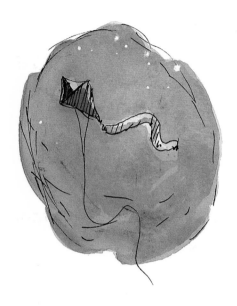

'TIL ALL THE STARS HAVE FALLEN

A Collection of Poems for Children

Selected by
David Booth

Illustrated by
Kady MacDonald Denton

PUFFIN BOOKS

For Marion Seary
D.B.

For George L. MacDonald
K.M.D.

PUFFIN BOOKS
Published by the Penguin Group
Penguin Books USA Inc., 375 Hudson Street, New York, New York 10014, U.S.A.
Penguin Books Ltd, 27 Wrights Lane, London W8 5TZ, England
Penguin Books Australia Ltd, Ringwood, Victoria, Australia
Penguin Books Canada Ltd, 10 Alcorn Avenue, Toronto, Ontario, Canada M4V 3B2
Penguin Books (N.Z.) Ltd, 182–190 Wairau Road, Auckland 10, New Zealand
Penguin Books Ltd, Registered Offices: Harmondsworth, Middlesex, England

First published in Canada by Kids Can Press Ltd., 1989
Published in the United States of America by Viking, a division of Penguin Books USA Inc., 1990
Published in Puffin Books, 1994

1 3 5 7 9 10 8 6 4 2

This anthology copyright © David Booth, 1989
Illustrations copyright © Kady MacDonald Denton, 1989 All rights reserved
LIBRARY OF CONGRESS CATALOG CARD NUMBER: 93-94985
ISBN 0-14-034438-1
Anthology title from the poem 'This I Know' from *The Salamander's Laughter & Other Poems*,
copyright © 1985 by Anne Corkett, published by Natural Heritage/Natural History, Inc., Toronto, Canada
Printed in Hong Kong

Contents

Introduction

As a child, I loved to read poems. I even took out the entire poetry collection from the children's section of the Sarnia Public Library—one book at a time, of course.

How fortunate I am to be part of this book, for I have been able to reread many of the poems from my own childhood and to discover so many delightful new ones that belong to your generation. I read hundreds of poems in preparation, and each one that I selected spoke to me in some way. I have tried to arrange them by whatever quality first touched me in the poem—sometimes the pattern that set my toes tapping, sometimes the pictures that flooded my imagination, sometimes the spirit that filled my heart, sometimes the memories that filtered through my mind, and sometimes the story the poet told.

Kady MacDonald Denton, the artist who created the wonderful illustrations that accompany the poems, read each of the selections and then filled the page with her own responses to the poetry, and her pictures dance and fly right off the page.

Poets are wordsmiths, spending their lives choosing, bending, shaping, teasing, playing with words. The sounds of language fascinate them so. Poets write words that make your ears sing. When you read poems, they come alive with out-loud language. You can sometimes taste the words of a poem on your tongue as you make meaning in your imagination.

Poets shape their words into all kinds of patterns: grouping them into verses, fooling with punctuation, twisting the lines like pretzel ideas. Sometimes the poem's shape can help you hear what the poet is trying to say.

Poets take photographs of our country, our seasons, our weather, our people and ourselves without camera or film—pictures worth a thousand words. You may find yourself in the photo albums created by poets—black and white memories.

Read the poems in this collection and share the illustrations that surround them. Let them touch you like the first snowflakes of winter. Savour them, feel them, wonder about them, and find some more of them. Reread them if you want to. Say them aloud. Read one to a friend. Laugh if you feel like it. Forget some of them. Memorize some of them. Don't pick them apart (that hurts a poem). Copy down the ones you enjoy the most. Leave out the ones you don't understand or don't like. (Come back to them later; give them a second chance.) Write your own poems — those who read poems often want to write them. If a poet connects with you, read a whole book by that poet.

I didn't write these poems; I just borrowed them to help build this book for you. There were so many to choose from, hundreds of years of poems — enough for everyone.

David Booth

1989

WHEN YOUR EARS SING

This I know

The light of day
cannot stay.
The fading sun
will not come
to anybody's calling.

The cold moon light
Is clear and white.
She will not go,
this I know,
'til all the stars have fallen.

Anne Corkett

Canadian Indian place names

Bella Bella, Bella Coola,
Athabaska, Iroquois;
Mesilinka, Osilinka,
Mississauga, Missisquois.
Chippewa, Chippawa,
Nottawasaga;
Malagash, Matchedash,
Shubenacadie;
Couchiching, Nipissing,
Scubenacadie.
Shickshock
Yahk
Quaw!

Meguido Zola

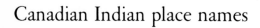

I get high on butterflies

I get high on butterflies;
the way they loom in the air
and land on air-dromes

               of petals

and with nervous wings
shake off their colours

               of orange, green and blue. . . .

I get high on butterflies;
their very names:

         Tiger swallow tail
         Zebra
         Pygmy blue
         Arctic skipper
         Spring azure
         Common wood nymph.

Caught in the net of my mind
they whirl around

            and around. . . .

Joe Rosenblatt

Nicholas tickle us

Nicholas Tickle us, make us all laugh,
   "I will if you pay me a dime."
Too dear, Nicholas, cut that in half,
   Just a nickel a tickle a time.

Sol Mandlsohn

The muddy puddle

I am sitting
In the middle
Of a rather Muddy
Puddle,
With my bottom
Full of bubbles
And my rubbers
Full of Mud,

While my jacket
And my sweater
Go on slowly
Getting wetter
As I very
Slowly settle
To the Bottom
Of the Mud.

And I find that
What a person
With a puddle
Round his middle
Thinks of mostly
In the muddle
Is the Muddi-
Ness of Mud.

Dennis Lee

Mischief City

A typical day in Mischief City,
The world's topsy-turvy, the world's out of whack.
They're looking at me and they're shaking their heads
And they say this all happened since I got back!

My name is Maxine, this is Mischief City,
Everything's damaged, soiled, busted or cracked.
My family is wishing they'd stayed in their beds
And I wish I could get my act back on its track!

My name is Maxine, *I'm* Mischief City,
I'm a runaway train that just ran out of track.
I'm a walking disaster, a giant whose tread
Leaves a trail of disaster, of ruin (and wrack)!

They're raising a statue in Mischief City,
It's a statue of me and my name's on the plaque.
I'm on top of this wrecking ball made out of lead
With a cloud overhead, and the cloud's painted black!

I've got to get out of Mischief City,
Before I reduce this old house to a shack.
I could move to the jungle, or maybe instead,
I'll just move in with you! Now how about that!

Tim Wynne-Jones

15

The sneeze

I winked and I blinked
And my nose got itchy
And my eyes all watered
And my mouth went twitchy
I went AHHHH
I went AHHHH
I went AHHHH CHOOOOOO
And I blew
And I sneezed
Then I coughed
And I wheezed
And my brother said, "Oh, brother!"
And my mother said,
"GAZOONTIGHT!"
My father said, "Bless you!"
And I said, Ah . . . ah . . . ah . . .
AHHHHHHHHHH CHOOOOOOO!

Sheree Fitch

The fox and the hounds

The fox
is happy he
is a fox

Except when
he is hounded
by hounds

The hounds
are happy they
are hounds

Especially when
they hound
the fox

When the fox
outfoxes
the hounds

He dreams
of being hounded
by more hounds

And the hounds
dream they are
those hounds

George Swede

Rattlesnake skipping song

Mississauga rattlesnakes
Eat brown bread.
Mississauga rattlesnakes
Fall down dead.
If you catch a caterpillar
Feed him apple juice;
But if you catch a rattlesnake
Turn him loose!

Dennis Lee

Basso profundo

A singer, who sang
   in a deep basso key,
Lived three miles down
   in the Sargasso sea.
"I know it is hard to breathe,"
   said he,
"But no one in the world
   sings lower than me.
Glub diddy dum dum,
   glub diddy dee,
No one in the world
   sings lower than me!"

Sol Mandlsohn

Sea cliff

Wave on wave
and green on rock
and white between
the splash and black
the crash and hiss
of the feathery fall,
the snap and shock
of the water wall
and the wall of rock:
after—
after the ebb-flow,
wet rock,
high—
high over the slapping green,
water sliding away
and the rock abiding,
new rock riding
out of the spray.

A.J.M. Smith

Coyotes

The coyotes are howling;
    it's forty below.
The moon is silvering
    shivering snow.

Keeⁱpipipipi^{ipipip}ipi_{pip}_{oo}

    kaiueoo oooo   yup
       eeee

eeee^{yayayayaya}

oooooooooooo^{ooooooo}ooooo ooooo^ooooooo^ooooo oo^{oooo}oo^ooo^o

                                ap
                            ap_{ap}
       puka_{aa}_{aa}_a   ap_{ap}
    kee_{oo}haha_{ha}   kyip   ap
           _{hahahaahaa}haa

    How many coyotes
    do you think there are?
        One for the moon
        and one for each star.

aueeeeooo^{ooooouiiiiui}wa^wa^wa^wa^wa_{wa}_{wa} ⁱ
                       aⁱaⁱaⁱaⁱⁱaⁱⁱaⁱ

   yute yiee_{yeet} yite
  eae_{ee}
     _{ee}^{eee}eeee_{eeee}_{ee}_{ee}eee^e

The coyotes are crying;
    the night is awake
with their crying at midnight
    on the frozen lake.

20
      Jon Whyte

A path to the moon

From my front door there's a path to the moon
that nobody seems to see
tho it's marked with stones & grass & trees
there's nobody sees it but me.

You walk straight ahead for ten trees or so
turn left at the robin's song
follow the sound of the west wind down
past where the deer drink from the pond.

You take a right turn as the river bends
then where the clouds touch the earth
close your left eye & count up to ten
while twirling for all that you're worth.

And if you keep walking right straight ahead
clambering over the clouds
saying your mother's & father's names
over & over out loud

you'll come to the place where moonlight's born
the place where the moonbeams hide
and visit all of the crater sites
on the dark moon's secret side.

From my front door there's a path to the moon
that nobody seems to see
tho it's marked with stones & grass & trees
no one sees it but you & me.

b p N i c h o l

21

IN SILENT SNOW

December

round slice of moon: December night
stark branches lift
from hollowed black to silvered white
    no wind disturbs

the stars swing by in frozen flight
soft smoke floats thin
from fires alight in rooms below
    the stillness holds

in silent snow
neat footprints write a winter's tale
    the night dreams on

Fran Newman

23

November

<pre>
                              sun
                              the
                              than
        Snow   higher
         and   fly
         night   geese
         comes   sky
         down   of
         into   ledge
          the   yellow
              last
</pre>

Anne Corkett

A tomato

<pre>
        t o m a t o
      a t o m a t o m a t
    a t o m a t o m a t o m a
    a t o m a t o m a t o m a t
    t o m a t o m a t o m a t o m a
    t o m a t o m a t o m a t o m a
    o m a t o m a t o m a t o m a t
    m a t o m a t o m a t o m a t o m
    a t o m a t o m a t o m a t o m a
    o m a t o m a t o m a t o m a t
    m a t o m a t o m a t o m a t o
    a t o m a t o m a t o m a t o
    o m a t o m a t o m a t o m
    m a t o m a t o m a t o m
    t o m a t o m a t o m
    m a t o m a t o m
    t o m a t o
</pre>

Colin Morton

24

yawn

you know
i think
my favourite
thing in
the world
is
a
YAWN
i mean
everybody
does it
even
lizards
and
crocodiles
and i bet
if we only
knew
how
trees and
dandelions
do it too

as a matter
of fact
i bet
that when
all those
little
dandelion
fluffs blow
away
it's because
the dandelion
parent had

a great
big YAWN

and do you
know what
else is
great
YAWNS
are catching
i mean
when you
YAWN
then everybody
(or just about)
around you
YAWNS
and it
doesn't even
hurt
what a great
thing to give
to the world
a
YAWN

i bet
if all those
soldiers lined
up
facing each
other from
all the
countries
everywhere
in the world
and they were

all mad at
each other
i bet that
if just one
of them
YAWNED
the whole
world would be
safe

or
just imagine
if some bully
comes up
to you and
wants to
start a fight
just imagine
after all
the tough
stuff
all the
pushing
and making
faces
just imagine
if
just when he
was going to
pound you
you let out
a great big
YAWN

well
if that

didn't stop
him then
even if
he hit you
his fist
would go
right into
the middle
of your
YAWN
and if you
wanted to
you could bite
it off
of course
you wouldn't
have to
'cause everybody
would be
laughing so
hard
the fight would
be over

now
if you sneezed
at the same
time
imagine what
might
happen
●

sean o huigan

25

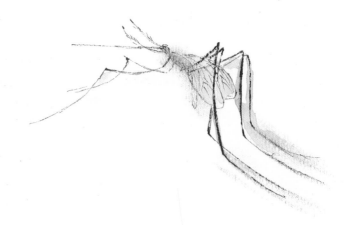

A mosquito in the cabin

Although you bash her,
    swat her, smash her,
and go to bed victorious,
    happy and glorious
      she will come winging,
      zooming and zinging,
      wickedly singing
over your bed.
You slap the air
    but she's in your hair
    cackling with laughter.
You smack your head,
    but she isn't dead—
    she's on the rafter.
She's out for blood—
    yours, my friend,
and she will get it, in the end.
She brings it first to boiling point,
    then lets it steam.
With a fee, fi, fo and contented fum
    she sips it
    while you dream.

Myra Stilborn

Holes

Holes are shy and dull and round.
They're nothing, but don't remind them.
They live in sweaters, socks and crowns.
In flutes and Swiss cheese, holes abound.
And they hardly ever make a sound.
And some end up in the lost and found.
But most are buried in the ground,
You have to dig to find them.
Holes.

Tim Wynne-Jones

My toboggan and I carve winter

My toboggan and I carve winter
We crunch over the powdery snow
the one by one glistening grains
they sigh and squeak

then RACE
faster and faster
whipping the wind apart
carving jet trails with swirling tails
circling the shadow of every tree
nearing full flight
til
WHOMP!
a lurking bump tumbles us
into the drifts of freezing snow
We trudge slowly skyward for another run

Jane Wadley

Why/because

Why   did

i
j
u
m
p

from

the

h
c oo
s   l

s
tep
s

t
o

t e
h

wb
o a
n   n
s   k?

Be
c
a
u
se

i

w
a
s

l   y
o   l

n e

Brian MacKinnon

The north wind

Once, when I was young I knew the wind.
I called "Wi-ind, North Wi-ind"
And it came,
 tramping the grass so that it lay flat,
And whinnied high and shrill like a whistle.
I saddled it with imagination,
 and bridled it with dreams.

And I got on and we went, and the trees
 bowed down in our passing.
I was exhilarated with the speed
 and lay down on his neck to keep
 balance.
And his snowy mane whipped about my face.
His unshod hoofs made no sound
 as he trod on the stars.
His breath made icicles on the houses
 we passed
And then he bucked.

Joanne Lysyk

HIGHER THAN THE SUN

Poems can give you

Poems can give you
double vision.
They make you see
the colours you feel
when you're sad,
the sound of a red,
red sunset,
the smells of happiness,
the flavours of the seasons,
Double vision
not blurred
but crisp as last night's snow.

Sandra Bogart

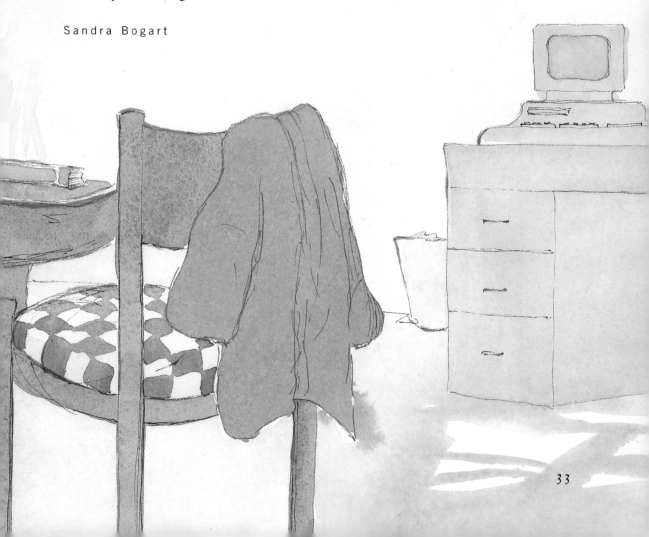

34

And my heart soars

The beauty of the trees,
the softness of the air,
the fragrance of the grass,
    speaks to me.

The summit of the mountain,
the thunder of the sky,
the rhythm of the sea,
    speaks to me.

The faintness of the stars,
the freshness of the morning,
the dew drop on the flower,
    speaks to me.

The strength of fire,
the taste of salmon,
the trail of the sun,
And the life that never goes away,
    They speak to me.

And my heart soars.

Chief Dan George

Think of the ocean . . .

think of the ocean
        as a cat
with her grey fur
            pushed
      high upon her back
        white boots
        kneading the shore
                on stormy days.

but
  with the sun
        shining
in a silk blue sky
       she purrs
  softly and her fur is
     licked smooth and green
like the sand stone
        she sleeps upon.

Siobhan Swayne

36

Fisherman

He is dark and wiry,
his bones, thin and sharp,
like the bones of the fish
in his net.
It seems as if
webbing grows on his fingers
and feet,
a starfish is his heart,
a seagull is his voice,
an oyster's pearl his eye,
he juts out of the sand
like a rock or some coral,
so long he has lived in the sea.

Dionne Brand

my friend

my friend is
like bark
rounding a tree

he warms
like sun
on a winter day

he cools
like water
in the hot noon

his voice
is ready
as a spring bird

he is
my friend
and I
am his

Emily Hearn

Hanging

High on the tree one apple alone
All her golden companions withered and gone.

Elizabeth Gourlay

Aesthetic curiosity

Does an owl appreciate
The color of leaves
As they fall about him
In the staggering nights of Autumn?

A.M. Klein

39

Jonathan's farm

I'd like a little farm
with a house that's painted blue,
with a lively little terrier
and a pussy cat or two.

I'd build a little barn
to keep my gentle cows,
outside I'd build a pig-pen
for piglets and for sows;

I'd plant a little orchard
with apple and with plum
and all the birds would praise
their green kingdom.

Miriam Waddington

October nights

October means it's Hallowe'en
When pumpkins don their faces,
And moans and groans and rattling bones
Are heard in haunted places.

When witches in their pointed hats
Go riding on their brooms,
And nighttime wears a velvet cloak
Of mystery and doom.

When graveyards start to come alive
With spirits of the dead,
It's such a lovely time of year
I think I'll stay in bed.

Harriet Cooper

Some winter pieces

Tiny figures stand
Frozen, still, on clean white snow.
Green ice pond, black trees.

So cold this morning,
Snow squeaks, crunches underfoot;
Steam ghosts dance on drains.

In my back garden:
Footprints of rabbits,
And a frozen dead starling.

Ice-coated maple
Groans slightly in wintersleep;
Yawns out one green shoot.

In late afternoon
Snow glows pink, pale sky burns cold;
Black shadows lengthen.

William H. Moore

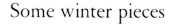

42

Winter yard

Bundled,
eyes watering against the glare,
we wade
into the crusty winter yard.
Bushes hang heavy
with suet-soaked onion bags.
Pine cones drip peanutbutter and seeds.
Coconuts hang by their eyes
and Javex bottles swing crazy
on the clothesline.
We smile
red tight
and closed with cold
and retreat to wait.

Shoulder to shoulder with cat at the window,
noses pressed on fogged-up glass,
we watch,
impatient.
Erin calls,
"Birds! Come here! We have seeds for you!"
Gulls sweep the sky.
Starlings crowd the neighbouring maples.
Jays scream.
Hundreds of wings beat the air,
and
    then
        they
            descend.

Norene Smiley

Laughter

We are light
as dandelion
parachutes we
land anywhere
take the shape
of wherever we
fall

we are often
the size of
grasshoppers in
a jungle of grass
or we're squirmy
chains of willow
catkins

then we become
curly seashells
knobby little
swimmers in a
sea of air
lying

on our backs
our eyes fly up
higher than kites
airplanes clouds
winds higher
than stars and

we stare down
at the little
distant world
and we laugh
laugh laugh

Miriam Waddington

44

Field in the wind

The grass is running in the wind
Without a sound,
Crouching and smooth and fast
Along the ground.
The clouds run too,
And little shadows play
And scurry in the grass
That will not stay
But runs and runs, until
The wind is still.

Floris Clark McLaren

The yellow tulip

For weeks
it struggled
through the hard crust
of the spring earth
and a foot
of air

Just to be
scorched
by the sun
jolted
by raindrops
blasted
by the wind

But on this gentle
May morning
as it opens
yellow petals
to the sky

Nothing else matters

George Swede

Silverly

Silverly,
    Silverly,
Over the
    Trees
The moon drifts
    By on a
Runaway
    Breeze.

Dozily,
    Dozily,
Deep in her
    Bed,
A little girl
    Dreams with the
Moon in her
    Head.

Dennis Lee

EVERYTHING IN ITS PLACE

Squirrels in my notebook

I went to Stanley Park
to put squirrels in my notebook
My teacher said
write everything you found out
about squirrels

and so I will

I saw a fat one
shaped like a peanut butter jar
attacking my hat

his moustache was made of chips
he ran sideways into the sky

He looked like a ginger cat
with a branch for a tail

He was so mad he ran down again
and I can't write
what he said to me

Lucky for me I had a sandwich
to share with him

He smiled at me till his teeth
weren't hungry
and jumped into the sky
with his jammy legs

he turned into
a kite.

Florence McNeil

Every morning

Every morning
I awake
full of dust
and odors

As if
no one has
lived in me
for years

And
every morning
I throw open
all my windows
and doors

Clean
and fumigate
myself

As if
I were just
moving in

George Swede

Courage

Courage is when you're
allergic to cats and

your new friend says can
you come to her house to
play after school and

stay to dinner then
maybe go skating and
sleep overnight? And,

she adds, you can pet
her small kittens! Oh,
how you ache to. It

takes courage to
say "no" to all that.

Emily Hearn

Tinkering

I love beginning with
a clean sheet and
laying down each grease-black
cog and bolt and link
aligning positions
adjusting tensions and
checking for wear.

I love finishing in
reverse order and
picking up each clean, oiled
sprocket, nut and washer
spinning the wheel
and hearing only the whirr
of everything in place.

Diane Dawber

Names don't always suit

Two cats live in the house
Across the street from us,
One cat is black,
The other is white.

At night I hear their owner
Calling them home.
"Coalbin," she calls the dark one.
"Winter," she calls the white.

But names don't always suit,
for Coalbin shines like silk
From washing herself,
And how can we call
Winter in summer?

Nancy Prasad

51

Jeremy's house

Jeremy hasn't a roof on his house
For he likes to look at the stars;
When he lies in his bed
With them all overhead
He imagines that he can see Mars.

Sometimes a thunderstorm lights up the sky
And Jeremy gets soaking wet;
But he says that it's worth it
To lie in his bed
And see folks go past in a jet.

He's counting the stars in the Milky Way,
It's going to take him forever;
But Jeremy's patiently
Counting away
For he knows it's a worthwhile endeavour.

Lois Simmie

Thrum drew a small map

Thrum drew
A small map

He put in
The small countries
The lizards and
The bugs and
The snails and
The worms

He made a mountain
And a green tree
And small rocks
And smaller rocks

He made a river
And a little fish

He made a meadow
And a little mouse

He made specks
That were ants
He made a queer smile
On the countenance of
A bee

He made a person
Small as a
Minnow

He made white birds
In a blue sky
But because he had no
Yellow
He couldn't draw the sun

He made an ocean
And a small boat

He made daytime and
Nighttime and a
Small evening star

He signed his name
In small letters
At the bottom
Almost too small
To be able to
See

He loved his small
Map
With its small
Small secrets

Grim came and tore it
Up

Susan Musgrave

Waiting for the first drop

No-one knows the exact moment
of what hour
the first drop of rain will fall.

But after one whole week
of blinding sun
of scorched grass
of wilting leaves,
it somehow seems important.

So I watch and wait
along with the birds,
along with the ants,
along with every living
breathing thing,

for that first heavy
cool splash of rain
to wet the page
of this poem about the rain.

Raymond Souster

55

Winter walk in forest

All else
is so
perfectly still
my breathing sounds
like gusts of wind
my joints
like frozen branches
cracking

All around me
invisible animals
must also be listening

But only
to how close
my boots
snap the snowcrust

George Swede

56

Recipe for Thanksgiving Day soup

today i made soup
on the woodstove—
with a snap of frost in the air,
a fire feels good—
    i started it off
with a soup bone
from the general store—
can't sell soup bones up here,
they give them away—this one
had great chunks of gristle
and beef on it
    —beautiful—
set it to simmer
at the back of the stove
in fresh water, threw in
onion and thyme from the garden,
a few celery leaves
bits of green pepper,
bay leaf, salt—
    it's the spring water brings out
    the goodness

meantime i filled up
the woodbox with stovelengths
i buzzed split and piled
from logs the neighbour's kid
    helped me haul up
from the gully
the woodshed is bulging

to get back to the soup—
while the stock was cooking
i diced up the rest of the vegetables:
    potatoes, tomatoes, carrots,
    a little more onion,
    peas, beans—
all grown thru the summer
and stored in the cellar—
    threw in a handful
    of wild rice
    for body
took out the soup bone, cut up
the meat and put it back in
saved the bone for
the neighbour's kids' dog

simmered the broth
to a rich autumn brown
    stirring occasionally
    with a big wooden spoon
    and tasting for flavour

called in the neighbours
to share it
we ate it with fresh
homemade bread
they brought over
    sure was good soup

Dorothy Farmiloe

57

The sky is falling

It's cool under the August
apple tree
and fun
lying on my back looking
at the sky
        shaped into blue chunks
           between leaves
       magnified
          between fingers
       rainbowed
          between eyelashes.
You can see a lot
everything but the apple
that hits your nose
and then nothing but
           stars.

Diane Dawber

Nature

As the orange-
striped cat
hunches,
glaring down,

the pale-fluffed
nestlings
he's discovered
feel cooled
in the shadow,

and

stretch their thin
necks, heavy
heads up,
hungry
beaks open,

wide
on hinges.

Milton Acorn

ALL MY SECRETS

If you don't come

The sun will get
smaller and smaller
and the grass won't green
or the trees leaf
and there will be
no flowers or birdsong.

The winds will blow cold
and the nights will be dark
without moonlight or stars

for there will be
no summer here
if you don't come.

Marguerite Mack

Fingerprint

My grandparents' kitchen
smelled of soap
            always soap
            and carrots

My grandmother performed
rituals in the kitchen
She had a man's hands
            but smooth
as if her fingerprints
had been worn down
levelled like old hills

My hands in her hands
working the soap
with a strong grip

Harry Thurston

62

Long, long ago

It seems I always saw the Indian woman
the instant she became visible,
and never took my eyes off her
as she lugged her many-coloured pack,
three times as big as herself,
down South Mountain,
across Little Bridge,
up North Mountain
and into our kitchen
where she undid a knot
and flooded the entire room with baskets
—cherry-coloured baskets,
wheat-coloured baskets,
cabbage-coloured baskets,
baskets the colour of a November sky,
each basket containing
another, smaller basket,
down to one so tiny it would hold
only a hang of thread and a thimble.

Alden Nowlan

Snake woman

I was once the snake woman,

the only person, it seems, in the whole place
who wasn't terrified of them.

I used to hunt with two sticks
among milkweed and under porches and logs
for this vein of cool green metal
which would run through my fingers like mercury
or turn to a raw bracelet
gripping my wrist:

I could follow them by their odour,
a sick smell, acid and glandular,
part skunk, part inside
of a torn stomach,
the smell of their fear.

Once caught, I'd carry them,
limp and terrorized, into the dining room,
something even men were afraid of.
What fun I had!
Put that thing in my bed and I'll kill you.

Now, I don't know.
Now I'd consider the snake.

Margaret Atwood

The roundhouse

That first real year
I pitched baseball
we played straight across
from the roundhouse on St. Clair,

and every time
I got jammed up good
in a three-and-two count,
I'd simply stall a little
till a black screen of smoke
blew across from its chimney,
then wind up and throw one
right down the gut
with no worries at all. . . .

But like everything else
that was too good to last—
the next year they tore down
my handy old roundhouse,
and I only finished seven
of my fifteen starts,

all the smoke gone forever
you might say
from my fast one.

Raymond Souster

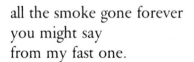

Together

Lying in bed
next to my mother.
This has to be the best,
the very best thing.
We are reading.
Dad is away
"Want an apple?"
and she bites in.
Crack, crack,
go her jaws
like a hinged fence
that doesn't work right.
I try not to listen
to those hinged jaws
I can't read
I've never noticed
my mother's jaws
doing that before
"Maybe it's the way
she's lying," I think to myself.
"Gee, you eat
apples funny,"
I finally blurt out.

She doesn't say anything.
She just looks at me
awful quiet
and puts the apple
on the bed stead
behind her.

We continue to read
in silence.

That was two years ago.

But it feels like
last night
the two of us
reading in bed

My mother
no longer eating
and I,
wishing, oh, wishing
wishing she were.

Carolyn Mamchur

The visitor

one night
i woke up
when the
rest were
asleep
and felt
something
crawly
that started
to creep
up my arm
'neath the
covers
i brushed
it away
but it
didn't go
it wanted
to stay
it creepy
crawled
slowly
with long
hairy
steps

it tickled
and
whispered
and got to
my neck
it sssssssed
and it hussssshhhhhed
and it sssssshhhhhhhhhed
and it haaaaaaaahhhhed
it creeped 'cross
my face
and it felt
very odd
it crawled
'round my shoulders
and crept down
my back
then spidered
away
and hid
in the
black

sean o huigan

And even now

When I was a child,
Lying in bed on a summer evening,
The wind was a tall sweet woman
Standing beside my window.
She came whenever my mind was quiet.

But on other nights
I was tossed about in fear and agony
Because of goblins poking at the blind,
And fearful faces underneath my bed.
We played a horrible game of hide-and-seek
With Sleep the far-off, treacherous goal.

And even now, stumbling about in the dark,
I wonder, Who was it that touched me?—
What thing laughed?

Dorothy Livesay

The royal visit

When the King and the Queen came to Stratford
Everyone felt at once
How heavy the Crown must be.
The Mayor shook hands with their Majesties
And everyone presentable was presented
And those who weren't have resented
It, and will
To their dying day.
Everyone had almost a religious experience
When the King and Queen came to visit us
(I wonder what they felt!)
And hydrants flowed water in the gutters
All day.
People put quarters on the railroad tracks
So as to get squashed by the Royal Train
And some people up the line at Shakespeare
Stayed in Shakespeare, just in case—
They did stop too,
While thousands in Stratford
Didn't even see them
Because the Engineer didn't slow down
Enough in time.
And although,
But although we didn't see them in any way
(I didn't even catch the glimpse
The teacher who was taller did
Of a gracious pink figure)
I'll remember it to my dying day.

James Reaney

Smart remark

When my older sister Marilyn
    came for a visit,
She spent most of her time trying
    to make us over
Into some other kind of family.
The kind you see on TV who get all
    excited and beam
Because they're having Lipton's
    Chicken Noodle soup for
    supper.
The kind who pick to spend the
    whole day in the new Mall.
The kind who love to do things
    together and talk non-stop.
The kind we aren't.
When she said, for the fifteenth
    time,
"Kate, must you always have your
    head in a book?"
The worm turned and I snapped,
    "Yes. I must.
It's better than having no head
—Like you!"

Dad laughed.
Mother sent me to my room.

Afterwards, she said,
"It was clever, Kate. It may even
    have been true.
But you didn't have to hurt her."

"She hurt ME!" I complained.
"Did she really?" Mother asked,
    looking me in the eye.
"Oh, I guess not," I said, thinking
    back over the visit.
"But she drove me crazy, picking at
    me . . . and . . ."

"You wanted to swat her," Mother
    finished for me.
"So did we all. But you don't swat
    butterflies, Kate."
"If she's a butterfly, what am I?" I
    demanded.
"A mosquito," my father joined in.
"But Marilyn's not exactly a
    butterfly, April.
She's more like a . . . tent
    caterpillar."

Mother laughed.
Why didn't she send HIM to his
    room?

I know why.
He said it when Marilyn couldn't
    hear.
In other words, behind her back.
Which makes him a spider?

And Mother . . . a . . . a . . .
Queen Bee, I suppose.

Jean Little

VOICES ON THE WIND

Orders

Muffle the wind;
Silence the clock;
Muzzle the mice;
Curb the small talk;
Cure the hinge-squeak;
Banish the thunder.
Let me sit silent,
Let me wonder.

A.M. Klein

Hurricane

Shut the windows
Bolt the doors
Big rain coming
Climbing up the mountain.

Neighbours whisper
Dark clouds gather
Big rain coming
Climbing up the mountain.

Gather in the clothes lines
Pull down the blinds
Big wind rising
Coming up the mountain.

Branches falling
Raindrops flying
Tree tops swaying
People running
Big wind blowing
Hurricane! on the mountain.

Dionne Brand

Windlady

Nine miles high
You drag me, your raindoll by
Till I've cried the rivers full
Windlady, weatherwinder, windsteeple
Windhat, windoldpaper, windowsill
Across the mountain, across the sea
     Wind me

James Reaney

74

My moccasins have not walked

My moccasins have not walked
Among the giant forest trees

My leggings have not brushed
Against the fern and berry bush

My medicine pouch has not been filled
with roots and herbs and sweetgrass

My hands have not fondled the spotted fawn

My eyes have not beheld
The golden rainbow of the north

My hair has not been adorned
With the eagle feather

Yet
My dreams are dreams of these
My heart is one with them
The scent of them caresses my soul

Duke Redbird

Zeroing in

The tree down the street
  has little green apples
    that never get bigger
     never turn red.
They just drop on the ground
  get worm holes
    brown spots.
They're
  just right for stepping on
    like walking on bumpy marbles,
     or green eggs that break with a snap
      just right for gathering
       in a heap behind the hedge
       waiting
        for a target.
Here comes my brother.

Diane Dawber

Here comes the witch

Here comes the witch.
    Don't make a sound.
Here comes the witch.
    Don't turn around.
Stand as still as still can be.
Like a statue, like a tree.
She's bony, warty, green-faced too,
Hungry for someone just like you.

Here comes the witch.
    She's very near.
Here comes the witch.
    She's now right here.
She's reaching out! She caught your eye!
Now raise your arms and *fly, fly, fly*!

Robert   Heidbreder

You better be ready

What are all those rocks sticking up for? he says.
Those are markers for graves.
Graves?
Where they bury people, after you die.
No, you are wrong, Uncle Johnny. When you die, God
    takes you away in a car.
Whereabouts?
Whereabouts?
Yes. Whereabouts does God take you?
It's a secret, he says.
Well, there are people buried right there!
I know, Uncle Johnny. But they just missed their ride,
    that's all.
Oh, I say.

John Lane

77

Licorice

For those who want the recipe
I give it to you here for free:
First you take a running shoe
And boil it for a day or two,
And when it's turned a greyish goo
You add the ink (in navy blue).
Erasers (lots), hairnets (a few),
Three rubber boots (two old, one new);
Then let the mixture steam and stew
At least one week (no more than two);
Then take a sieve and strain it through
And let it cool; in three days chew
And if it doesn't quite agree
Send me back the recipe.

John Paul Duggan

Unicorn

Unicorn, Unicorn,
where have you gone?
I've brought you some silver dew
out of the dawn.
I've put it in buttercups
for you to drink
and brought you some daisies
to wear round your neck.

Silver and gold
and petals so white,
these are the colours
saved from the night.

Unicorn, Unicorn,
where have you gone?

I've brought you nine sunbeams
to wear for a crown
and made you a blanket
of new thistledown
embroidered with lilies—
O where have you gone?
Unicorn, Unicorn,
I can't stay long.

Petals so white
and silver and gold,
these are the colours
that never grow old.

Anne Corkett

July

Lie on your front in the summer sand;
Bake for as long as you can stand.

Lie on your back, let the heat soak in;
Then roll around on your summer skin.

Lie on your side to enjoy the view;
Ease yourself over to toast side two.

Run to escape the blazing sun . . .
It's too late—you're overdone!

Fran Newman

80

Anxious

Anxious
of course I'm anxious
afraid
of course I'm afraid
I don't know what about
I don't know what of
but I'm afraid
and I feel it's
right to be.

Miriam Waddington

81

WHISTLING IN THE DARK

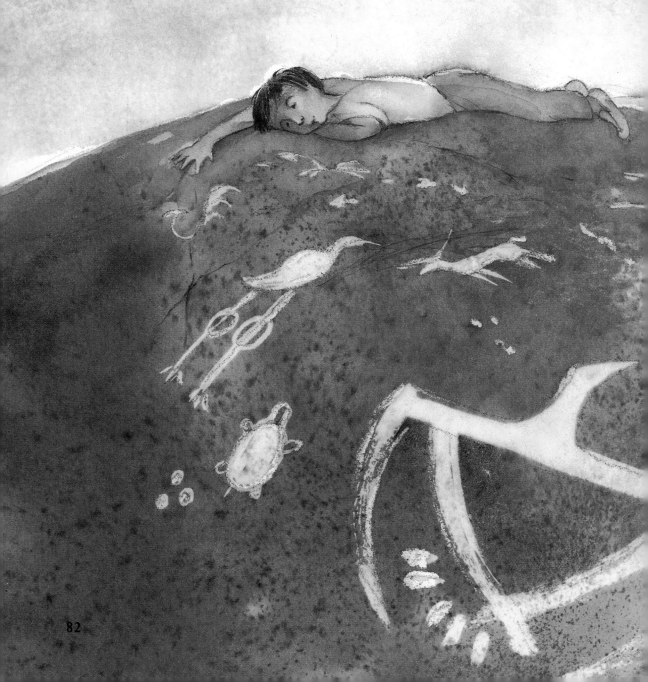

Drums of my father

A hundred thousand years have passed
Yet, I hear the distant beat of my father's drums.
I hear his drums throughout the land,
His beat I feel within my heart.

The drums shall beat, so my heart shall beat,
And I shall live a hundred thousand years.

Shirley Daniels

Too hot to sleep

He was sleeping when bear
came down from the mountain
by the water trap
after cleaning the screen
of branches and gravel

He fell asleep, a hot june morning
above Wapta Lake, the Kicking Horse Pass
When Muskwa came down without a sound
And snuffed at his jeans

Who's this asleep on my mountain?

It's my friend Birnie asleep I said
(in my head)
I didn't hear you coming bear
I was dozing, I looked up
and there you were

You never know said Bear
just where the wind will lead me
when I'll be around
or what beat I'm hunting on

and sniffed at Birnie's collar
at his ear, which he licked tentatively
causing Birnie to moan softly

Nothing doing here he said, nothing doing

"We were just going bear," I said quietly
edging backwards

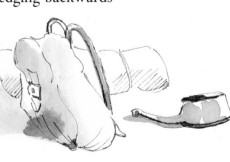

Don't move too quickly will you, said Bear
when you move, or better still
don't move at all

Are you here often, are you coming again?
he asked, flipping over a stone
licking delicately the underside
"No," I said. good he said, that's good.

I just came down from the pass
the wind blowing up my nose
to see who was sleeping on my mountain
he said, and sniffed at Birnie's armpit
Whoosh   whoosh he snorted

and turned away, clattered down the creek
popping his teeth, his hackles up
Went out of sight
around the shoulder of Mount Hector

as Birnie woke rubbing his eyes
"Too hot to sleep he said." Yeah.

Sid Marty

85

The dinosaur dinner

Allosaurus, stegosaurus,
Brontosaurus too,
All went off for dinner at the
Dinosaur zoo;

Along came the waiter called
Tyrannosaurus Rex,
Gobbled up the table
'Cause they wouldn't pay their checks.

Dennis Lee

86

Trip to the seashore

We drove to the seashore,
My ma and pa,
Brother Bertie
And Sue and me;
From Biggar, Saskatchewan,
Over the mountains,
What did we see?
We saw the sea.

Sister Sue said
"Isn't it big?
It's bigger than Biggar
Or anything yet."
Brother Bertie
Up to his knees,
And Ma to her ankles
Said "Isn't it wet?"

I let out a yelp
When I saw kelp
And a scuttling crab,
Pa laughed at that;
He sat on the land
With his toes in the sand,
"I'll be darned," he said,
"Isn't it flat?"

At the seafood restaurant
Ma had oysters,
They looked horrid,
Green and squishy;

There were boats through the window,
Sue had scallops,
(Pa said we had to have
Something fishy).

Bertie had lobster,
I had crab,
We looked through the window
At waves and foam;
Pa had whisky
And fish and chips,
He said, "We've seen it,
Let's go home."

We drove all day
We travelled all night,
The parents and Sue
And Bertie and I;
We fought over comics
And seashells and Pa yelled
"Look at the mountains!
Aren't they high?"

We got home to Biggar,
Ma and Pa,
Sister Sue
And Bertie and me;
Pa said "Look,
Isn't it beautiful?
Big and flat,
Just like the sea."

Lois Simmie

Windigo spirit

The Windigo is a spirit of the North, the Cree told us.
The Windigo is a cannibal spirit, the Cree told us.
The Windigo will possess a man
        form ice inside his soul
        cause fur to cover his skin
        create a craving for human flesh
The Cree told us,
Two bitter nights ago.
Two nights ago, we left their dismal camp, to check
Our traplines. It was twenty-below-zero
Two nights ago, but now it has gotten
Really cold. Windigo, Windigo,
Passing through our thoughts
Like wind at thirty-five below.
Windigo.
The Windigo moves thru the five moons of winter
        shrouded in a blizzard
        blown by high winds over frozen lakes
        or creeps inexorably on
        thru those still days
        when life is locked immutable in minus
        fifty skies, those cloudless, breathless
        days when neither air nor man dare move.
The Windigo crosses a portage
        then a sun-blind lake
        then the soul of any fool
        alone
            out here,
                like us

Now.
Two nights out, out from another man, we are still
Strangers in front of our fire,
        our meek fire melting
        melting just enough
        night air
        to breathe.
A shadow moves.
Windigo.
Two nights ago, the Cree told of a trapper lost,
Near here,
Now surely, host of
The Windigo Spirit.
Cold.
Windigo. Windigo.
Two nights out, the dead trapper enters the ring of our fire
        his own lips and fingers chewed off in hunger
        a gaping chasm of a mouth ringed with frozen
Blood.
Two nights out, I turn to my companion,
        behind his eyes ice forms
        his hands are matted with hair
This night, I rise and scream.
My scream crosses the frozen lake and dies somewhere in the
spruce
        dies somewhere in the spruce.
Windigo. Windigo.
Windigo.

Ken Stange

89

Paul Bunyan

He came,
striding
over the mountain,
the moon slung on his back,
like a pack,
a great pine
stuck on his shoulder
swayed as he
talked
to his blue ox
Babe;
a huge, looming shadow
of a man,
clad
in a mackinaw coat,
his logger's shirt
open at the throat
and the great mane of hair
matching, meeting
the locks of night,
the smoke from his cauldron pipe,
a cloud on the moon
and his laugh
rolled through the mountains
like thunder
on a summer night
while the lightning of his smile
split the heavens
asunder.
His blue ox, Babe,
pawed the ground
till the earth
trembled
and shook
and a high cliff

toppled and fell;
and Babe's bellow
was fellow
to the echo
of Bunyan's laughter;
and then
with one step
he was in the next valley
dragging the moon after,
the stars
tangled,
spangled
in the branches of the great pine.
And as he left,
he whistled in the dark
like a far off train
blowing for a crossing
and plainly heard
were the plodding grunts
of Babe, the blue ox,
trying
to keep pace
from hill to hill,
and then, the sounds,
fading,
dying,
were lost
in the churn of night,—
and all was still.

Arthur S. Bourinot

90

91

Acknowledgements

Grateful acknowledgement is made to the publishers, authors and other copyright holders who have granted permission to reprint copyrighted material.

Every reasonable effort has been made to locate the copyright holders for these poems. The publishers would be pleased to receive information that would allow them to rectify any omissions in future printings.

- "This I know", "November" and "Unicorn": From *The Salamander's Laughter & Other Poems* by Anne Corkett, copyright © 1985. Reprinted by permission of Natural Heritage/Natural History Inc., Toronto, Canada.
- "Canadian Indian place names": By Meguido Zola. From *Here Is a Poem*, published by the League of Canadian Poets, copyright © 1983. Reprinted by permission of the author.
- "I get high on butterflies": From *Top Soil* by Joe Rosenblatt, copyright © 1976. Reprinted by permission of Press Porcépic Limited and the author.
- "Nicholas tickle us" and "Basso Profundo": From *Nicholas Tickle Us*, published by PMA Publishers, Toronto, Canada, copyright © 1985 by Sol Mandlsohn. Reprinted by permission of the author.
- "The muddy puddle": From *Garbage Delight* by Dennis Lee, copyright © 1977. Reprinted by permission of Macmillan of Canada, A Division of Canada Publishing Corporation.
- "Mischief City" and "Holes": From *Mischief City*, copyright © Tim Wynne-Jones 1986. A Groundwood Book, Douglas & McIntyre. Reprinted by permission of the publisher.
- "The sneeze": From *Toes in My Nose*, copyright © 1987 by Sheree Fitch. Reprinted by permission of Doubleday Canada Ltd.
- "The fox and the hounds": By George Swede. From *High Wire Spider*, Three Trees Press, copyright © 1986. Reprinted by permission of the author.
- "Rattlesnake skipping song": From *Alligator Pie* by Dennis Lee, copyright © 1974. Reprinted by permission of Macmillan of Canada, A Division of Canada Publishing Corporation.
- "Sea cliff:" From *The Classic Shade* by A.J.M. Smith, copyright © 1978. Reprinted by permission of the Canadian Publishers, McClelland and Stewart, Toronto.
- "Coyotes": By Jon Whyte. From *Prairie Jungle*, edited by Wenda McArthur and Geoffrey Ursel, copyright © 1985. Reprinted by permission of Coteau Books, Regina, Canada.
- "A path to the moon": From *Giant Moonquakes and Other Disasters*, copyright © 1985 by bp Nichol. Reprinted by permission of Black Moss Press.
- "December" and "July": From *Sunflakes and Snowshine*, copyright © 1977 by Fran Newman and Claudette Boulanger. Reprinted by permission of Scholastic-TAB Publications Ltd.
- "A tomato": By Colin Morton. From *Here Is a Poem*, published by the League of Canadian Poets, copyright © 1983. Reprinted by permission of the author.
- "Yawn:" From *Well You Can Imagine* by sean o huigan, copyright © 1983. Reprinted by permission of Black Moss Press.
- "A mosquito in the cabin": By Myra Stilborn. From *Round Slice of Moon*, copyright © 1980, Scholastic-TAB Publications Ltd. Reprinted by permission of the author.
- "My toboggan and I carve winter": By Jane Wadley. From *Round Slice of Moon*, copyright © 1980, Scholastic-TAB. Reprinted by permission of the author.
- "Why/Because": By Brian MacKinnon. From *Here Is a Poem*, published by the League of Canadian Poets, copyright © 1983. Reprinted by permission of the author.
- "The north wind": By Joanne Lysyk. From *Pandora's Box*, published by The Canadian Council of Teachers of English.
- "Poems can give you": By Sandra Bogart. From *Round Slice of Moon*, copyright © 1980 Scholastic-TAB Publications Ltd. Reprinted by permission of the publisher.
- "And my heart soars": By Chief Dan George. Copyright © 1974 by Chief Dan George and Helmut Hirnschall. Reprinted by permission of Hancock House Publishing Ltd. 19313 Zero Avenue, Surrey, B.C. V3S 5J9
- "Think of the ocean": By Siobhan Swayne. From *Here Is a Poem*, published by the League of Canadian Poets, copyright © 1983. Reprinted by permission of the author.
- "Fisherman" and "Hurricane": From *Earth Magic*, copyright © 1979 by Dionne Brand. Reprinted by permission of the author.
- "My friend" and "Courage": By Emily Hearn from *Hockey Cards and Hopscotch*, copyright © 1980 by Nelson Canada. Reprinted by permission of Nelson Canada.
- "Hanging": From *To Say the Least*, copyright © 1979 by Elizabeth Gourlay, Press Porcépic Ltd. Reprinted by permission of the author.
- "Aesthetic curiosity" and "Orders": From *The Collected Poems of A.M. Klein*, copyright © 1974. Reprinted by permission of McGraw-Hill Ryerson Limited.
- "Jonathan's farm": This poem appears in *Collected Poems*, copyright © 1986 by Miriam Waddington, with the title "Child's Poem". Reprinted by permission of Oxford University Press.

- "October nights": By Harriet Cooper. From *Here Is a Poem*, published by the League of Canadian Poets, copyright © 1983. Reprinted by permission of the author.
- "Some winter pieces": By William H. Moore. Published by permission of the author.
- "Winter yard": By Norene Smiley. From *Seaweed in Your Stocking*, copyright © 1985. Reprinted by permission of the Children's Writers' Workshop.
- "Laughter" and "Anxious": From *Collected Poems*, copyright © 1986 by Miriam Waddington. Reprinted by permission of Oxford University Press Canada.
- "Field in the wind": From *Frozen Fire*, copyright © 1937 by Floris Clark McLaren.
- "The yellow tulip", "Every morning" and "Winter walk in forest": By George Swede. From *Time Flies*, Three Trees Press, copyright © 1984. Reprinted by permission of the author.
- "Silverly" and "The Dinosaur dinner": From *Jelly Belly* by Dennis Lee, copyright © 1983. Reprinted by permission of Macmillan of Canada, A Division of Canada Publishing Corporation.
- "Squirrels in my notebook": By Florence McNeil. From *Here Is a Poem*, published by the League of Canadian Poets, copyright © 1983. Reprinted by permission of the author.
- "Tinkering", "The sky is falling" and "Zeroing in": From *Oatmeal Mittens*, copyright © 1987 by Diane Dawber, Borealis Press. Reprinted by permission of the author.
- "Names don't always suit": By Nancy Prasad. From *Here Is a Poem*, published by the League of Canadian Poets, copyright © 1983. Reprinted by permission of the author.
- "Jeremy's house" and "Trip to the seashore": From *Auntie's Knitting a Baby*, copyright © 1984 by Lois Simmie. Reprinted by permission of Western Producer Prairie Books.
- "Thrum drew a small map": From *Gullband* by Susan Musgrave, copyright © 1974. Reprinted by permission of Douglas & McIntyre.
- "Waiting for the first drop" and "The Roundhouse": By Raymond Souster. From *Flight of the Roller Coaster*, copyright © 1985. Reprinted by permission of Oberon Press.
- "Recipe for Thanksgiving Day soup": By Dorothy Farmiloe. From *Here Is a Poem*, published by the League of Canadian Poets, copyright © 1983. Reprinted by permission of the author.
- "Nature": By Milton Acorn. From *I've Tasted My Blood*, copyright © 1969, McGraw-Hill Ryerson Limited. Reprinted by permission of the estate.
- "If you don't come": By Marguerite Mack. From *Alberta Poetry Yearbook*, 1975.
- "Fingerprint": By Harry Thurston. From *Barefaced Stone*. Fiddlehead Poetry Books, Fredericton, copyright © 1980. Reprinted by permission of the author.
- "Long, long ago": From *Bread, Wine and Salt*, copyright © 1967 by Alden Nowlan. Reprinted by permission of Irwin Publishing, Don Mills, Ontario.
- "Snake woman": From *Interlunar*, copyright © Margaret Atwood 1984. Reprinted by permission of Oxford University Press.
- "Together": By Carolyn Mamchur. Published by permission of the author.
- "The visitor": From *Scary Poems for Rotten Kids*, copyright © 1982 by sean o huigan. Reprinted by permission of Black Moss Press.
- "And even now": From *Collected Poems: The Two Seasons*, copyright © 1972 by Dorothy Livesay, published by McGraw-Hill Ryerson. Reprinted by permission of the author.
- "The royal visit" and "Windlady": From *Poems*, copyright © Canada 1972, by James Reaney, published by Press Porcépic. Reprinted by permission of the author.
- "Smart remark": From *Hey World, Here I Am*, by Jean Little, copyright © 1984. Reprinted by permission of Kids Can Press Ltd., Toronto, Canada.
- "My Moccasins have not walked": By Duke Redbird. From *Red on White: The Biography of Duke Redbird*, by Marty Dunn, copyright © 1971. Reprinted by permission of Stoddart Publishing, Don Mills, Ontario.
- "Here comes the witch": From *Don't Eat Spiders*, copyright © 1985 by Robert Heidbreder. Reprinted by permission of Oxford University Press Canada.
- "You better be ready": By John Lane, from *What Are Uncles For*, Harbour Publishing, copyright © 1985. Reprinted by permission of the author.
- "Licorice": By John Paul Duggan. From *Here Is a Poem*, published by the League of Canadian Poets, copyright © 1983. Reprinted by permission of the author.
- "Drums of my father": From *I Am an Indian*, copyright © 1969 by Shirley Daniels.
- "Too hot to sleep": From *Headwaters*, copyright © 1973 by Sid Marty. Reprinted by permission of the Canadian Publishers, McClelland and Stewart, Toronto.
- "Windigo spirit": By Ken Stange. From *Here Is a Poem*, published by the League of Canadian Poets, copyright © 1983. Reprinted by permission of the author.
- "Paul Bunyan": By Arthur S. Bourinot. From *Watcher of Men: Selected Poems 1947–1966*, Hurtig Publishers Ltd.

Index of authors and titles